100 P O E M S

John Moat

100 POEMS

John Moat

PHOENIX PRESS

1998

The Publishers

6d per Annum, Phoenix Press
Thunder of Grass, Barrie & Rockliff, The Cresset Press
The Welcombe Overtures, Dartington Poetry Press
The Ballad of the Leat, Arc
Fiesta & The Fox Reviews His Prophecy, Enitharmon
Firewater & The Miraculous Mandarin, Enitharmon
Practice, Libanus Press
Skeleton Key, Typographeum
The Valley (with drawings), Libanus Press

© John Moat, 1998
Photograph of John Moat by Andrew Lawson

Phoenix Press
Hermitage, Newbury
Berks RG18 9XR

ISBN 0 900852 19 4

Designed and typeset in Bembo
at Libanus Press, Marlborough
Printed in England by Smith Settle, Otley

CONTENTS

From *Firewater & the Miraculous Mandarin*

Takes in his fingers
The porcelain leaf

Makes a bird in the heart
And weeps for the tree

Shows where sky lingers
Though seasons are brief

Knows how to depart
And leave the house free.

From
6d per Annum
Thunder of Grass
The Welcombe Overtures

Infidelity

I'm endeavouring, love, to write the tenderest words
Ever a poet turned to song.
But find in thought a dustiness as if
I'd been away from my work in happiness too long.

Strange, I've never experienced a love so sure,
Or seen so clear the heart of the simple few
And yet it seems months since I worked with my pen.
It was yesterday. I spent the whole of last night with you.

In my garden

In my garden for some days now
Flits the shadow of my bird
In the dark beyond the massive leaves
Of my magnolia tree he
Cheeps. But through the night he
Alarms my neighbour so
Shrieking about the things he knows
And how he is wedded to the worst in me. He
Spoils my work which means all life to me
With his fretful fluttering.
If only he would understand I care for him but O
Would rather black my soul than set him free.

Reverie for child and garden
I. M. Doctor H. Holtby

I

I inherited the garden towards dawn
And keep it with a very moderate art;
Though this may prosper now a child is born
To simplify complexities of heart:
The toil is simple while the love is one;
Two kids would tear a toiling soul apart.
For charity I work a routine spell
As premium to save my brat from hell.

2

I must allow the loneliness of pain,
The isolation of the frail desire,
The grand desire's inscrutable disdain
That grants its double-dealing with the mire.
But when there's clamouring in a common vein
From that fond world bewildered by the fire,
Then shall I offer kinship in her fear,
And for the child's peace exercise my care.

3

I kneel before her little golden boy
To claim participation in his birth;
I suckle him on all my rampant joy,
And breathe the milky perfume of his breath.
She scolds me then because she thinks I toy
With unearned ecstasy beyond my worth . .
But Love, Oh Love, hasn't my birthbone cracked,
And earth's sore opening my labour slaked?

4

Yet even as I kneel I seem to doubt
Desire's prepared to toddle with a child –
My will, self-gratifying, paints the drought
The colours of a garden rank and wild.
Then splendid creatures hang their baggage out
And drule how dreamers have their love defied
By priests who grudge high-summer's plenty,
First snare the soul, then leave the garden empty.

5

At evening I have the clearest sight
Of the real directors of my garden's life.
As birdsong softens and the querulous light
Subsides, so all the inmates of my daily strife
(the tout, the tramp, the over-perfect knight)
Withdraw, and then the gardeners arrive
With delving learned beyond time-torn repose
To tend my child, and bud my blighted rose.

Overtures

Just now in my hut I woke up. Out in the valley Fred
Was bellowing like a bull. I thought, 'He's gone off his head.
He's never been this angry before. Perhaps it's a dream.'
Then I remembered I'd seen the cows, out from the milking
    shed,

Stand and chew the air as if for a thought. Then turn and walk,
Heads down, swinging their hips in the sun, off up the stream.
I should have known. Up in that meadow for days Arthur's been
Digging, and planting out the young greens. Enough said.
The drills hoofed in, the peas munched down to the stalk.
It won't be milk tonight in the churn – it'll be cream!
I stand to watch the procession come back.
Procession? Stampede. The cows skip and gallop at the head,
Lowing, their udders awallop, and the excited dogs aswing
On their tails, and last Fred running and cussing and waving
    a fork.
Still, look who's in luck – caught napping by work.

*

I sat beneath the dim photo of Uncle Bill
In his prime in gaiters. Beside me on the sill
The cat purred and clawed the lace. We all chewed in time
To the slow clock in the kitchen. The quiet was full
After the yammer of the tractor and the hayrake.
Or when the tractor stopped by the rick there'd been the stream
And the swift sound of hayforks in dry grass. Long sunshine
Had left few words and little thought, only an equal will
To sleep or work. It seemed to me that blood could take
The same green sweetness from the sun as the crisp hay. By signs
We asked for pasty or more tea. We chewed and let the clock
    make
Up the time. Fred sat up. We listened. A chuckle
From the sunlight outside the door, a little whine,
And then again a chuckle. The Missis smiled. 'They'm come
    awake.'
Old Bill and the cat – playing hide and seek.

*

So much for your open road
On a shoe-string knotted to God
Your slippers under your bed
And next month's oats unsowed
Your star groans in the sky
For a single prayer unsaid,
The rim of heaven is red
And you'll no more abroad.
The hero stops with a sigh,
Marks where some Caesar bled,
Stops and then passes by
And carelessly shoots his load.
The hermit in his shed
Munching his humble-pie
Carelessly waves good-bye.

*

There have been times recently when I've gazed
At her (most often it's been when our eyes
Have suddenly met, I watching, but she, caught,
Seeming to listen, in an indecision of ways,
Looks at me sharply, inquiring, then softens,
Maybe lets the teatowel drop
Or gathers her hands shyly into her lap —
Though not always) and there seems a haze,
Though not about her face, and the room darkens,
Though not about her face, and I've thought
How when identity is most clear often
We are singly not alone, and how then flesh —
Its definition — is transparent, inapposite,
And I've known that I'm caught up in a poem
Which is under way — but which won't ever be written.

*

She wore before all was begun
The bathrobe of the setting sun
And flames ran thrilling everywhere
The many-coloured waters run.
A whisper mentioned to a lace,
Let loose the evening light of hair –
At last it glimmered on my chair
The fallen nightdress of the sun.
The stars will claim the pride of place
To lay the nightly downland bare,
And dark bees swarmed about my face
And where the moontide waters ran
And scent of lilies filled the air
I tasted me all night's embrace
While dark bees swarmed about my face.

*

Whatever's happening in our flesh
The wind of change becomes my wish
Isolde sleeps and now I may
Put the sword back in its sheath
I touch her bodice as we smile
Each dwelling on a single lay
A white dove is an act of praise
A promise is a silver fish
I take her fingers for a while
And feel a strangeness gone away
And on another strangeness build
The dream that's flooding in her breast
We breathe and breathing is to pray
That we can bring to winter cold
The oneness of this summer child.

*

I stop the mower. The cat's asleep on the wall
Like a pink muff. In the loft the doves grumble
At the heat. The tortoise breaks from a bed and turns
Crotchetty across the lawn. The two retrievers growl
Or snore on their backs like drunks sleeping
It off where the shade has inched them into the sun.
Butterflies light on the buddleia, bees thrum
Into the blue. And silent around and over all
Is our house – not a dream, but silence spilling
Out of the open windows where the blue curtains hang
Quite still. Somewhere inside she is sewing.
Does she hold up the thread to listen I wonder? I call
And the silence confers. My love, we've made home,
Take my hand. Now listen. Strange on a summer evening
To hear the gulls at the end of the valley start screaming.

                    *

Christmas Eve the blackbird started carolling,
Two months back, tricked by the stillness, by a lingering
Moment before dark and the sudden mild, into the song
He keeps back normally as a surety of spring.
I was in my hut, heard it and held my breath. Since when
The snow has come and lain forgetful on the fields, and gone –
And still the blackbird has never held its tongue.
Soft light this evening in the garden, and the murmuring
Of warm rain. One daffodil now. And the blackbird again
High in the blue firtree. He sings. And then for some
Time he listens as if for reply from beyond the rain,
From a silence that is in from the sea, or beyond, listening
For where the diffuse quiet should end in confluent song.
I watch from the porch him tilt his head. Then he's off again,
Trilling, carolling. And somewhere in the house the whisper
    'Amen'.
                    *

I listened to the singing all along
When perhaps I should have listened to the song
Perhaps it was another song she sang
And I and what I like to think was wrong
How could I know until the song was sung?
Perhaps it was before the song began
That I'd decided how the wording ran
Perhaps presumption never does belong
Once the actual measure is begun
But when at length I saw that she still sang
And for all her wasted labour had not clung
To any still-born rapture of the song
Then I took heart and fashioned with my hand
This little poem out of all she'd sung
And so redeemed sad God what He had done.

*

The heron creaks over and up the stream, he's
Got the frost in his joints. Wonder he clears the trees!
But if he's stiff he's still on his way, off to fish some place.
Ice this morning on the step, ice on the milk. The last leaves
Gone from the sycamore, a few stragglers left on the oak.
But the great cherry . . . The cherrytree's still ablaze.
Orange and brazen and yellow. Twice yesterday from the house
I thought the sun broke through. But no, just a cold breeze
Flashing the cherrytree. And whenever it shook
A leaf would fall, or two, and the cat was there to chase
And juggle the leaf like a flimsy mouse. But today, from
    my books,
I see they've begun to fall – no wind, just the yellow leaves
Falling and falling in a silent shower. Ever noticed

In mid-winter when the leaves have gone how the water
  will talk?
In summer a reticent stream – in winter a brook.

*

Beloved, what am I to do? In the night a spider
Has slung his web between the keys of my typewriter –
The A, the & and the ?. Then I'll pick up the windfall thread.
John Keats, coughing his own sentence, produced the rider
That man may like a spider out of his own innards weave
His own airy citadel. That's strong thread.
Love, I'll give you this: I believe in what he said.
The utterance is sole earnest of the creator.
And his heart the vein of joy that cannot come to grief.
And suffering? Who knows – crust on the daily bread?
But I know flowering is all, and joy the sap of the tree.
The tree I graft today grows from the Gita,
A figtree rooted in heaven whose trunk and branches spread
Out into existence, and there, prayers in the wind, the leaf
And flower: your eyes, my poems, our house, our child,
  our breath.

*

The pebbles are out of order. Some man's
Been down to meddle with the stones again.
On all the wide mindless beach this one thought
Breaks out to spoil the sea's unthinkable design.
He's been building, stone lifted onto stone.
No one else on the beach, and he builds a fort –
To live with himself. Sandcastles and forts
And wailing walls and burial mounds – and then
At sundown, after the last man has gone
From the shore, the sea moves in without a thought

And smooths the beach. And now the builder has gone
And the patient sea is on the move again.
It smooths the pebbles into place, and the thought
Falls into place. And I, the last thought standing alone,
Am drawn to the peace that will follow when I too have gone

Winter Passage

Going and coming I seem to have sat still
Here in the valley since last gasping June,
And all the long winter, even abroad, this waterfall
Sounding in the back of my mind.
A drought first, somewhere in September,
So the water falling was scant and slurred,
Muddled with the first stir of wind
And lipped syllables of falling leaves;
Some days sounding within the sea mist
That drifted up from below the cliffs
Where that time sullen waves emerged from calm,
Mounted in silence and turned over at last flashing distantly
To fall and echo in the green stillness
Of their own tumbling caves.
And sometimes still fainter under muffled land mist
Which, autumn, stays in the hollows until dinner,
Pearled from above by the last cloudless sky.
A nor'wester carried off the final leaves
And then some frosty days the brittle fall
Tinkled syllabic in the valley
Like china and the fine talk at Sunday tea.
October the first hard frost, and next day
The old heron flew upstream on his yearly round,
Stiff, his flight seeming quite silent,

Though his slow wings appeared to clatter
Leaving the valley quieter still,
And the stream's trickle deliberate, more remote
Like the voice beneath a child's window
Repeating some grown-up nonsense to itself,
Heard in the last flimsy moments
Before the child falls asleep.
November rain recharged the stream
The day I set South following a trail of sun,
Faint at first, more recent in spain, down to Morocco,
Coming eventually back to the sound of the waterfall
In a mountain valley east from Marrakesch
Not a waterfall in fact, a brilliant river
Plunging down over pink boulders from the snow not
    far above.
The valley sides were banks of a rushing sound
And the torrent itself submerged in this rare resonant ether
Until I hear nights only impermeable silence,
Can see only sunlit trees, olive, poplar, eucaliptus
Bend just and shimmer in a noiseless wind,
And will sit beneath the moving shade,
Cool, its silence full of patterns
And the mingled voice of the river.
                    *
On the far bank in the sun a field of corn.
In the blue shade of a tree a small girl tends a cow.
She stares idly, then across at me shyly, then idle again.
A brown sheep trots behind.
They move into the sun.
A baby hung in a pale orange shawl clings to her back.
They both stare at me from over the river.
The girl in an olive green blouse,

And orange and green flowered skirt to her ankles,
A broad bright yellow belt and green boots.
She has gold rings in her ears. Her face is brown,
Her hair and eyes darker. A pale blue head scarf –
Each colour single against the yellow
And green leaf and the blue shade.
  I have travelled here, and from now
  I'll stare back at the saint and the sage
  And stand between them and this world
  Since I've seen how the spirit before sleep
  Claims substance only in the factual loveliness
      of things.
  And will stake my lot and life on what is frail
  And bound to die
  And blossoming in spite of everything
  Beside this holy river sprung from Atlas snow
  To flow in all faith from the mountain
  Out onto and out in the dry terrible sand.
                    *

Home in December it took some days for the involved ear
To distinguish from so much memory
The full fluency of the mid-winter fall.
By now it had begun to freeze.
No wind, but the silence complete as the frost set in
And the third measure began to make itself felt.
Now with no leaves left the tinkle of the stream
Was anvil-edged;
With no wind and of birds only the robin
To cheep for an hour before dark,
The hammering was set out in tense relief
From silence.
And then beyond the silence this third measure

Which mid-winter's day is like the sensed breathing
Of something asleep.
For a week it froze, some mornings sunlit agleam,
Others dull, and all the time the tinkle was growing finer,
More metallic and stainless, and the silence more positive,
Reaching it seemed further out from the valley,
Even over the sea which just then was cold and sluggish.
Meantime that third element of sound or quiet
Seemed minutely more nearly audible.
Icicles began to form at the sides of the fall.
As hour by hour the trickle diminished
They encroached on the single flow
Until at last what was left of the stream
Sidled down one great needle of ice
To fall singly onto a mound of ice beneath,
Each drop a note in the valley
Clear as a coin dropped in a plate.
The stream has frozen —
And if ever silence was open to the eye
It is here now,
Clear cold and still in the nub of ice.
The poet gone to his hut an hour ago,
Sat beyond the frosted window motionless
And now his eye is no longer listening.

*

I've moved up-river to where I can see the girl more
clearly.
I sit down on a rock and pretend to dream.
She sings to her sheep
And through the tremendous sound of the fall
Her words come over to me
And they are mine.

She has seen me move.
She is older than I remember,
And the child is her son or her brother,
A rude laughing boy with a shaved scalp.
She cuffs his ear and he runs
To hide in the tall corn,
Dancing and laughing at the rudery.
The girl turns.
It is a woman's walking for me in the green silk
And under the shock pink shawl
Down to the river's rim –
And a woman's eyes lowered from noticing mine.
She bends down to the water.
As she washes her hands they linger over each other.
Still bending she undoes the half veil from her brown face,
Stands and looks about her vaguely,
Turns and walks away
Until she is no more than a movement
Among the moving shadow of the olive trees.
    And now that I may I state she is singing
    And though I shall never hear the sound
    Know it is included with the voices of the tumbling river
    That flows for ever between her and me,
    Whose echoes are the underflow of this waterfall
    Bucketting now in Spring spate,
    And the lambs bleating on the hills.
    With such a tune at the back of my mind,
    With the white baying hounds cantering past our house,
    The summer to come,
    I sense I now have the hand
    To draw the river over the terrible sand
    Down safe to the sea.

Stages of Solar Eclipse

Alone again now, needless, and she become
No more than a sleeping partner, familiar and remote
As the to do that just now woke me, caught
Us up and for a time in the mum
Of night made one of us of a need for song.

After – she retreats in sleep into other arms;
I hold her, she sleeps, her live lips mouthing less
To my cheek. Onement of sleep is not loneLness;
I wakes to loneliness, thinks, hears a farm
Dog out in the dark yelp from a falling churn,

The wind in the bamboos move – a moth just,
Or a bat, sees the stars free-falling above;
Walking alone he conceived the stars, his love
In splinters he cast out onto the outer dust
Of loneliness. We see stars because he must.

Alone again now I begin to wonder. She sleeps.
Our double bed is consummate. Now her dreamless breath
Is reduced to sleep self-contained as death.
Man is the eye awake; but before, asleep,
Was woman with an after smile on her lips.

The stream in the dreamless hour is her measure.
Unconceived it can work on sleep. It draws sleep together
Into images. The stream out loud tonight
Infects the cipher with a formal appetite.
Soon in the dark one bird will flash up the river.

A corncrake calls. I alone can see the bird,
Record its silent flight in my mind's eye,

Register on a scanning ear its one lonely cry
As it veers into the woods. Seen and heard.
Or does the waking eye project, the ear utter the word?

Were we born into sleep and forgetfulness?
All that fluttering! I think Wordsworth misread
The paradox, as though he viewed it standing on his head.
It's the lonely eye reflects unconsciousness,
While dreamless sleep is perfect holiness.

Her smile disquiets me here, what with stars for company,
And all this aching and heart-beat in the night.
I react to it as to the dark the light.

Confounded by her self-sufficiency
I mouth with God his first word, enmity.

First then was waking and sleeping
In one bed; the finger and the untouched string.
The lonely finger moved out of necessity
And plucked a measure for eternity.
Dryden was wrong. Need was first. Then came the song.

Years I've juggled with this chicken and egg,
To drop the clutch at full stop of one line,
"What in God's name lies between sleep and dream?"
Last week two soloists strung a bridge in my head.
Now I have the Almighty tucked up in a double bed.

Imrat playing the sitar on a moonless summer night,
The dark of the moon, quite mindless, touches the strings
And lets the music and his occasional laughter ring
The silence. Heart ordered the music, finger replied:
A mastered spontaneity to anticipate the mind.

Light isn't from his eye, but about the face.
It is the parted lips, lids, the fold in the dress.
The lids touch, the image dissolves within the caress
No longer Krishna's fingers, it is Radha's uplifted breast;
The bees come home to the blossom, annihilate in taste.

Jean Rudolphe-Kars has the fingering by heart.
Outside the open window a blackbird sings in a tree.
The premeditation forgotten, hammer responds to key.
Strings are struck. Eye overlooks the melody, as taught
Fingers respond to appease the ecstatic heart.

Light isn't from his cold eye, but in what he hears,
Bending over the board he listens and sees;
The moment of performance contains its memories
And tantrums all annulled. Webern strums, catches at the air.
Cold eye the still; the sounding ether has him by the ear.

In this hemisphere I am in loneliness:
Cold eye, prompt finger signing the paper;
Midnight oil to justify the hunger;
Beethoven slamming the piano to bits; proud humourless
Logic sentencing his own pretty sister to the cross.

While over there sense is underhalf of prosody.
Vidyapati rhymes Krishna to his place.
Eye overcome, thoughtless, faces her unveiled face.
"Shyness dropped with my clothes," she breathes. "My body
Hid my body. Krishna I saw everywhere!" Perfect euphony.

A double bed. Between sleep and dreams an unutterable word.
Yes and no. Either way I bend to Siva and his ridiculous dance,
Take his timing to heart, dispel the cold light at a glance.

So above the dark movement of the stream flashes the bird;
Deep in our timeless bed a moment stirred.

Less asleep she moves closer. Mind picks up the heart.
Two distant hearts. Detached, it records their movement on
    my bone;
Awake, asleep, mine faster. Each a beat on its own.
Out in the night we are the beating of our hearts.
But what if between a third movement start!

Child – a golden ring on a girl's finger,
Given and received; one fact of absolute duality.
Thought in the marriage of minds, pearl of unanimity,
A promise – promising nothing but a limited future;
Its tense the contracted present, unpredictable tinder.

But the best man has to offer. The word itself is a promise -
Soft light on the terrace, the girl
Looks up and is momentarily surprised by the Angel,
Catches her breath; from there the sentence is autonomous,
The two may worry, but the child will find his own way to
    the cross.

And still the fact remains. That night the movement slowed,
You singing in the labour ward, and came to an end;
"A child born dead," you said, then you ordained,
"A child is born." Unspeakably true. Meaning lives in a word;
The promise keeps alive where meaning is preserved.

Not deep-frozen, but alive – nourished in changeable air.
Put a promise on ice and the flavour is gone:
Frigid Novalis content, weeping on Sophie's tomb.
But two lovers, bite about, eat the last apple to the core.
What remains? "Where on earth now?" Just as before.

While the promise holds good. And why so much on surmise?
Because that's in a word, an illegible condition.
But break faith and, O brother, you go it alone.
After the fall Milton's God promised Adam a rise.
The second word revived him – he opened his eyes.

Eve had been right to accept nothing on credit;
Faith is rediscovered in the logic of each moment,
So now was high time to fall for the serpent.
Like a true wife she invited Adam to share it,
Their love came alive perceiving them naked.

Psyche too, laid out for a monster, had a curious suspicion
When carried away by blind Eros, into his bed.
She put up the light. He fled –
Blustering, calling her names. Still Psyche was forgiven
And by her illumination they were reunited in heaven.

One hour ago I turned on the light in her eyes,
Directly beneath mine, aglow, no trace of commotion,
But not dead or sleeping, simply overcome;
Their light naked, preoccupied
Anew by the ceremony of bridegroom and bride.

Loneliness above became tight-strung,
In danger of her eyes. Now suddenly it catches light
And sees this moment come round night after night
And never recur, because time always intervenes to bring
The central fact forward to a new setting.

Knowledge, each moment, is the clue to fidelity;
And faith – an agnostic's peculiar vapour;
The word given and received is a heroic venture,

Penelope's little thread runs right through the Odyssey,
The calling of the unknown is the proof of their constancy.

Word – a golden ring on a girl's finger,
Given and received, fact of absolute duality,
Child between man and wife, theme of unanimity,
A promise, promising nothing but a limited future,
Following a single clue, the Son – or a daughter.

There is light not from the stars now, out in the silent blue.
Somewhere a bird wakes, startled by his own first note.
She shivers, turns over, draws the blankets up to her throat.

Outside wind, first rustle of day, ruffles the bamboos,
A girl, come of age, in green taffeta and dancing shoes.

Ushas, sister of night, lovely mother of the sun,
Changeable and . . . John Donne, I smile and am prepared
    to swear
I can this moment lay hand on a woman true and fair.
And cold eye, in first cold light, thinks he can apprehend
The wind that serves to advance an honest mind.

Here now, in face of change, I prove that arresting art
Can pin all space down to this point in our bed,
Can for the prospective child create a launching pad –
So this moment Love, I again put hand on heart,
Even as one night's gas of stars is guttering out.

And I contract to him the future and the stars.
Each moment we'll set a station to disprove that hope
Probes only a blind eye far end of the telescope.
Looking in your eyes just now I saw,
Quite clear within the moment, Omega.

Night's thin coda on the stream has now begun
To submit to mounting pressure of birdsong;
Daylight from our window sets your eyelids just
Questioning the standard measure of your breast;
Night lies disarrayed before the rising sun.

Now soon the sun will break from the topmost branch
To set, my love, our double bed aflame.
Morning has come round again.
Now we dismiss the cold light at a glance.
Come, true heart, get out of bed — and dance.

From
Skeleton Key

I sing this autumn
after mid-summer's dying, before I turn cold
to mid-winter's desolate wisdom.

I may not write verse better than this. September
is colours of the earth, is beaten gold.
Sunlight conceals the patina.

For me all that is certain
is in shadow. She is alive – in the gold,
in the harvest, in the torch-light procession.

*

Sweat from the sky –
the love-sweat. I have sweat blood,
sheet-blood, the red hood to the vulture's eye,

The crumb-fat quivers,
Life feeds it, picked from the rood
it feast on joy. The gristle gathers

to heal, sweat, bleed – and die.
Life is exquisite. Drink then. The drop is good.
Drink the cup dry.

*

Creaks the heron's wing, leaves
from the lonely cherry falling into place,
the other trees

all bare − and just yesterday, Look!
the brazen cherry flashed ablaze
when the cold wind shook.

Now and not a breath
her leaves fall to lips which, long summer days,
could not catch the brook's brief.

*

He looks away,
can no longer hear into the stream's
winter cipher my voice at play.

There isn't a voice any more,
no shadow; he dreams
but no dream gets up from the floor.

The girl's gone away
into the olive shade. It seems
she'll not be back. Who knows? I may.

*

Her name escapes me; the leaves,
there yesterday, are fallen. Frost −
and the winter beast breathes

slow to not mist the glass,
the last sound is lost,
held beyond thought in the third eye of ice;

and coldly he sees
a girl, not a ghost,
come bodily from the shade to bind the sheaves.

*

Brown Arab girl other side of the river
in blue olive shade
and mingled measure

here's the run of my life,
of this strange double bed,
five-roomed house and my one chosen wife,

O brown-eyed woman, stay over the river
in the shifting shade
and mingled measure.

*

In sleep I came aware
first of the dull
beat beat beat drumming me into her power

And then the night running red
Until I no longer feel the tide-pull –
I am the flood.

The sky's a shower
of stars, the moon is full,
and the jacaranda in full flower.

*

An empty embrace.
I'm dark in his arms like the moon's shadow
I am his emptiness.

Until his glare
Lights the absence out of me. I glow
To his sense of my being here.

His face
Is morning – the bed full of him, of me too,
And both lost in this, our first kiss.

*

All afternoon she slept – the weight
of summer, the syringa
scent, the stream withdrawn in the heat.

Evening the air stirred.
We had grown old. At full flower
the petals fell, and the song-bird

turned to the cold wind. Our love is dust, is consummate.
The stream's sound is clear.
Our eyes meet.

*

After rain
the valley will brim with birdsong.
In the orchard the mole is digging again,

his hill mountains. Water
envelopes the earth. I have longed
for a child – can hear his laughter

down by the tense stream –
and nearby her clear voice, against the storm
and the gull's distant scream.

*

A cold north wind has begun to blow.
Summer is through,
Harvest's child already below.

Ice fines the air.
Winter's hour belongs to the few,
the blossoming of the world laid bare.

High-flier clouds like the wild geese go
through the distant blue
from Arctic to Antarctic snow.

*

I am the darkness – Alpha.
With darkness I fall,
the dragon abroad, the dreams appear.

I am the pinnacle –
I tumble and the shadows call,
tear the veil in the temple.

I am Omega.
As he wakes, the smoke drifts from the hall –
dreams and the darkness clear.

*

*Breath is ceremony, is leaf to the bole; but life unpolished
is unbearable – until
a stone brings up the burnish.*

*As if a vizor of gold must shield the eyes
from so much violence. But are you meanwhile
alive? You have aged. But not your eyes.*

*I see nothing diminish.
I imagine your smile.
You are alive in the gold, and gold will not tarnish.*

From
The Ballad of the Leat

For Arthur, Dolly and Fred

'And His voice as the sound of many water.'

First then – Arthur Beer who has lived at Watergap
now on seventy summers and farmed
to a farmer's share of storm
and sun, learning how to bend with the sap

better each spring, each winter keeping warm,
and all his life well clear of the sea
except twice and then didn't stop but got on home to tea,
though he can listen to it any night the air is calm

and the surf down the valley running on the rocks as he
back from The Anchor finds his way to bed,
or stands out the back of the old shed
for a final fag under the blue firtree,

he has said
(I looked by at their kitchen door on my way
to work to see what he might say,

the Missis there frying the bacon and bread,

letting it burn as she tried to think back too) that it were a day
before his day that they built our mill;
though he could recall the last one to work the wheel,
and that a while before Doctor came,

John Cam, evenings when he was back from the fields,
a youngster then with yellow hair
and dolloping arms, dead now a good few years,
and forty odd when he got finally ill.

With him gone, Edward Knight, the old miller
('ad a black beard,' was all Arthur could recapture of him)
packed it in
(I guess the broken mill-stone was the final straw).

And so by the time Doctor came
and bought up the land
and started collecting every flat stone for a mile around
to build each moment of his spare time his walled garden

Arthur's cows and the bramble roots had already broken
    down
the sides of the leat, and the stream had washed away
the head-dam past any
repair short of building it over again.

The bed of the leat was already dry,
the water had ceased to flow,
the oak axle to the mill wheel, twelve inch thick, rotted
    through –
Doctor meant to have it working again one day

but for the moment he had plenty enough to do,
enough to keep him and Jack Fulford his builder tied
up thirty years. In fact it was the day he died
(Jack, incidentally, is the undertaker too)

he was at last ready to go ahead
with the dam, the walls complete, the leat as well,
in the garden that is, together with bridges and waterfalls.
Afterwards his second wife, who, I've heard it said,

had had about her fill of building walls,
though she too had loved the place, seeing me come along
and fall for it, agreed to let me buy it for a song,
'rather than let some heathen in: Harold would never rest at all!'

Increasingly, as time went by, and I lived here alone,
usually in summer, standing outside the door,
breathing the evening after a hard day, I'd be aware
that something sounded wrong,

or not quite right. At those times too the Doctor,
whom of course I'd never met, would seem to me
so much alive that if I turned my head I must see
the old man bending over his rose. Simply he was there,

and in the end I took his company
for granted; I felt that we had conversation
discussing whatever he thought needed to be done.
The way I sweated he was no mere fantasy

But always the thing he was on
about (he or the loose nerve flickering in my head)
was the fact that wild celery and flag had choked the bed
of his leat, which he'd built so he could hear the water run.

*

I remember the hay was new-mown,
by the wall the tall orange-scented syringa
just breaking and the honey-suckle in flower,
the night air like breathing syrup and about to drown.

Out of the valley the sea was gently turning it over,
deliberate but subdued, as if it broke
on a shingle beach, and not bare rock,
the sound distinct and distant, picked up from a nearby star.

Closer, and somehow cryptic in the overgrown dark
on either side of the garden, the two
streams kept up an intermittent patter, their flow
reduced by the long drought to a trickle.

But the garden itself was still, as though
breathless; only occasionally, like a deep
sigh, or something shifting in its sleep,
would the darkness move in the bamboo.

I'd been touched, the sun maybe, and now the final leap:
my pulse fell in measure with a quick tread of shoes
on the lawn, slippering the dew.
On the room's dark, yellow and green came glancing up

like sunlight in a wood. I put my head in the pillow.
But the light stayed, and suddenly the thrash and splatter
as the full head of water,
plunging from the mill-pool into the wheel hollow

took up on the oak buckets, then all the clatter
and racket of the machinery, the wooden cogs
straining, the creak of pegs
and the stones turning. Of course later

it was easy enough to see what had nudged
me over the rim: a day's sun, a night on the ale
and then to put a lively head on it Arthur's tale
about the evening old man Bailey took his nag

and cart delivering flour and left him to mind the mill.
Just one sack of grain and the work would be done.
There was evidently, above the wheel, a flat stone
that acted as sluice gate in the pool

(the pool being the reservoir which, if one
shut down the stone last thing, would fill over night
with power enough for the next day, handy during
    a drought
when the stream was low). 'And what then?' I asked. 'I been

and got the stone stuck,' Arthur said. He had started to shout
but no one heard, and anyway the din
was terrific because he'd shifted the stone in
such a way more water than was meant was bucketting out.

He ran up the hill to Cranham Farm for help. But no one
    was in.
And by the time he got back
the miller was home, standing shock still with a sack
on each shoulder, fair jiggered out of his mind.

The cogs were straining fit to break from their brackets,
the wheel still crashing round, though by now the pool was
    almost dry.
What did old Bailey say? Arthur smiled: 'He didn't bide
to ask nort, he set to and laced me to the truth of music.'

                    *

That night when we'd cleared away Antoinette and I went
    to bed
early. I felt strangely dejected and irritable;
the air was like a dozen blankets, hot as hell.
The windows were open. Outside

the garden was silent, utterly still,
and far away the sea turned over in the night,
derisively, I thought. Then suddenly the sky caught light
and seemed to explode, flashed blood-red and fell

about our home. We lay there and held each other tight
and listened to the deluge and the thunder.
I closed my eyes to pray, since clearly the house was going under.
Next thing I was staring out of the window at a bright

heaven of stars. The air was cool. But the chief wonder
(and Antoinette grabbed my hand)
within the roar of the streams there was another sound,
unfamiliar but quite distinct, and since it wasn't louder

than the streams, it was apart, more intimate, more finely turned.
The water was plunging over the fall
into the mill pool
and even as we listened we heard

the new metallic note as it spilled
over the dam and ran under the stone
steps. Soon the entire garden
was sounding to the leat as fall after fall

took up the theme, each to its own tune;
and finally the bass descant as the water flowed out
under the wall. We lay and listened long into the night,

and when I slept my mind was full of sunlight and brown

moving shadows and the flash of rainbow trout.

*

That October came a new hazard, falling leaves.
They stuck and formed a block somewhere beneath
the road. The water piled back, overflowed, broke out

through the gates and appeared bent on Watergap hearth.
I ran up to dam the leat-head, while Fred at the double
fetched his sweep's brushes. Together we sorted out that trouble.
Midwinter did bring a small parcel of grief.

We lost a child. By the time Antoinette was home from hospital
the valley was frozen stiff. Snow on the hills, but in the hollow
just ice. For three days the streams continued to flow.
Then they froze. The leat too. And now the silence was total.

So still in the valley I could actually hear the fizz of the snow
overhead, and a mile downstream at Strawberry Water
Mr Oke cough. Beyond – there was the endless murmur
of the leaden sea, and now and then the tow

under the cliffs as it pulled on the pebble shore. But much nearer,
as if in some private silence, the intermittent creak of ice.
When Spring came finally, it seemed to come in a trice,
the daffodils we'd planted the summer

before bobbing and bowing on the leat banks
above the clear spring water. This year, from the end of May,
the summer was wonderful, hardly a day's
rain or sea-mist, and those hot summer nights

Fred found he could use the leat in a new way
to cool the milk. Until the leat gave out.

This year when the drought
came something strange happened . . . No, enough to say

it happened, and that I took note.
I'd been working (on this poem in fact) but when
the leat ran dry, I too – dry as a bone.
It was as if the bone had stuck in my throat.

I worked often enough, but it was late autumn
before I could put my finger on another word.
Since then? Well, the leat has been running at full flood.
Except today. Today I've had trouble with the leaves again.

I spent the afternoon prodding under the road.
But just now I was able to call by on Arthur,
in the kitchen, sitting by the fire,
and repot that all is well. He gave a slow nod

and smiled, and the Missis said she were used to that water
and didn't care 'tall for it when 'ms quiet. As I walked on up
through the orchard to work the frost crunched under foot. I stopped
on the bridge for a while to listen to the clatter

of the streams. They are loud tonight, and clear. But
there's no wind and so in the darkness I can hear
also the sea; the waves break with the crack of gorse-fire,
and then a boom that rattles the door of the hut.

But I was saying that on the bridge just now, as I stood there,
idle, and listened and watched my breath cloud
the stars, it suddenly occurred
to me that I've not been aware of the Doctor so much this year.

For a moment I felt scared. But then wondered –
isn't that what I might have had wit to expect.

I started. From somewhere upstream I thought I caught
the sound of a child's laughter. I turned. Nobody there.

It's late. Down in the house Antoinette
will be fuming as the supper dries up.
A long day, still here's an end to it. I hope
she forgives me when I hand her the leat.

From
The Fox Reviews His Prophecy

The fox stopped for a moment
called for a glass of real ale
one sip and he spat the drool on the floor
while a ghost-horn sounded the kill

He grimaced − but then he relented
'Now for the good news,' he said
'These last hundred years have upset the sun-cart
the utopian dream is dead.

True the white ants are into the larder
the reds raven under the floor
but the season they work is Nature's Springtime
it's the Forest's foot in the door

True the bowel-movements are still regular
in Kremlin and County Hall
where nine-to-five bureaucrats go through their motions
that don't touch the living at all

True up and down the country
still grinds the assembly line
where mice from the standard housing-estate
clock into the rat-race at nine

But under the standard winding-sheet
fade one or a million lives
and though pockets still jingle in Old Broad Street
the pantheon revives

The mind fed fat on his logic
is heavy and obese
see him try to hopscotch on white bone stumps
now worn to above the knees

Out in the English hedgerow
a young man sleeps in the grass
Arthur sits up, yawns, rubs his blue eyes
and winks at you as you pass

Out in the English meadow
a young woman sleeps in the shade
Britannia stirs, stretches, beckons to you
the nut-brown dairy maid

Children born deaf to the cash-till
hear ancient poetry
the data-bank's shelved for a rule of thumb
called self-sufficiency

The supermarkets tumble
throughout the bartered land
the selling trade-mark is the imprint
of the human hand

The juke-box plays second fiddle
publishers join the dole-queue
Medici the banker reads in his ledger
the renaissance is overdue

Behind the budding woodland
hear the woodpigeons tell
how the simple turn of the furrow shows
our inheritance is well

Out in the summer twilight
under the new harvest moon
the true daughters of memory come out to dance ... '
The landlord let out a moan

The landlord groans. He strikes the bar.
'Time gentlemen please!'
The fox leaps down nimbly from his hook on the wall
is off back to his earth in the trees ...

And the New Moon Is Her Face

*A song-drama for two voices
and a chorus.*

First Voice: November foreshore is the barest place on earth.
The sea in time will pick over any bone – even the bones of
memory. Even a ghost's bones. The heart goes out of them.
Sea-wrack remains. Between here and Crab Rock – tar,
debris, a broken doll. A lone limpet. The place is empty.

> The sea gleams her warning
> White breaker, white race
> The ground-swell is moaning
> Rain shadow in showers
> One memory cowers
> An old moon is her face

Second Voice: The yacht reached the Tarry Sound at evening.
No wind, we came in on the motor. Peter at the helm, I
astride the bow. The water running clear as a slow mill-stream,
mackerel deep down like silver leaf in a sudden breeze. The
scent of gorse drifted from the island, sweet as coconut.

> I bought her the morning
> White ribbon, white lace
> The sea's hem was foaming
> Her skirt was white flowers

Her island all ours
And the new moon her face

And in the wave's trough
Or when the light comes through the downspill
        of a breaker
A sound like laughter

Or caught up in the moment of its breaking
Between the wave-crest and the torrent of
        its falling
I see a shadow.

First Voice: Sick to death. Eager for death. A man mid-life
waits for the tide to turn. 2.35, a mile to the Northwest, a
yacht beats to the lee of the Burrough – a broken gull in
a green squall. No shelter there – the island torn open.
The song-birds migrate at the knell of summer: flamingo, the
bird of paradise . . . she has flown.

        The sea gleams her warning
        White breaker, white race
        The ground-swell is moaning
        Rain shadow in showers
        One memory cowers
        An old moon is her face

Second Voice: The path up from the jetty was a carpet: pine
needles and pink shells. At some point I caught the blue smell
of wood-smoke. And that other scent. She had gone up the
path to the house a few minutes before. The evening was so
still. Maybe that moment I fell in love. Though the first
meeting came later.

I bought her the morning
White ribbon, white lace
The sea's hem was foaming
Her skirt was white flowers
Her island all ours
And the new moon her face

And in the wave's trough
Or when the light comes through the downspill
        of a breaker
A sound like laughter

Or caught up in the moment of its breaking
Between the wave-crest and the torrent of
        its falling
I see a shadow.

First Voice: The day darkens. Though still, the sea shows white
down to Razor Rock – bares its teeth. This gale grates on old
bones. Night comes down on the Burrough. They have put
out the light. The sea's face wiped clean. Time to return,
revive what's left of the fire. Dreams start at midnight.

The sea gleams her warning
White breaker, white race
The ground-swell is moaning
Rain shadow in showers
One memory cowers
An old moon is her face

Second Voice: She told how seeing me on the path, coming as
in a dream, she hid. Afraid, not of the meeting but . . . some-
thing remembered. One blue flare, like summer lightning – a
whole life-time consumed. But when she heard me on the

stone terrace, she came out. I turned. She stood in the door-
way. She had caught the sun. She was wearing a white dress.

> I bought her the morning
> White ribbon, white lace
> The sea's hem was foaming
> Her skirt was white flowers
> Her island all ours
> And the new moon her face.

And in the wave's trough
Or when the light comes through the downspill
    of a breaker
A sound like laughter

Or caught up in the moment of its breaking
Between the wave-crest and the torrent of
    its falling
I see a shadow.

First and Second Voices (a canon, the second echoing the first):

> The sea gleams her warning
>   I bought her the morning
> White breaker, white race
>   White ribbon, white lace
> The ground-swell is moaning
>   The sea's hem was foaming
> Rain shadow in showers
>   Her skirt was white flowers
> One memory cowers
>   Her island all ours
> An old moon is her face.
>   And the new moon is her face.

Fiesta

'We have seen that while for the European there were ceremonial *occasions,* for the subjected Indian *life itself,* the very act of existence, was an act of cult, immersed as it was in the disproportionate miracle of cosmic logic.'   *Francisco Salmerón*

This Day Will Go on for Ever

All night the dead have been gathering
these are the dancers
los negritos, the moors, the men in skins and the white men

up in the cactus field
fire explodes around the statue of Our Lady
the dead wait

at sunrise they will put on their masks
the dogs and the *burros* rave
the cocks are crowing

here is the conquistador on his horse
the dead begin to dance
the happy house opens its doors

43

a girl in a print frock sweeps the earth patio
glances up at the taut sky
the coral tree is in flower

this day will go on for ever.

The First Fiesta

This the first fiesta
the *tepo* drum
the sky stretched over the mountains
the drummer on horseback somewhere over the land's
rim
a wave on a wave
a white bird
he comes he is coming
the earth is alive to his drumming
the one with the white face
the *gringo* come with the woman in the moon
Jesus and Mary
now we will sleep a thousand years
dance the ghost dance
dressed in yellow feathers
we put on the costumes of the dead
the marigolds in the graveyard
where the living lie buried
we are the sleeping dancers
we are the yellow flowers on the graves of the dead
as if the sun shone for us
we dance

We have forgotten.

The White Face

The moon was not enough
half in the dark

They prepared a meal
the shadows came, all the gods

The moon too *Perhaps she'll bring enough light*
but it wasn't enough
The witchman sang
Dig the pit, light a fire
There was a boy, his face white
he had been chosen
I am ill, I am nobody
They gave him feathers, a god's-eye
a gourd of tobacco
They put him in the fire
the night lasted five days
Then the sun shone
it was the first dawn
We bring firewood, cornbeer
all day the sun shines
The moon has gone, and the thousand masks
there is only the one face
The white face
And about the grave
the yellow flowers.

The Emergence of Sin

The sun broke out
there were no shadows
the bush clicked in the heat
outline was liquid
a figure seemed to have emerged
the world simmered
around the white face

The figure withdrew
and
the figure remained

But it was like turning the page
or removing the mask
or unveiling her face
or simply closing one's eyes
to shut out the sun
the figure remains
and the face is black

La Conquista

The ceiba tree is dead
the centre of life
we have lost heart
we are ghosts

The *hombre* with the white face
he is lord of the dead
why should we fight with him
we will dance beneath his cross

We will cling to the colours of life
the quetzal feather, the mask
we will dance
and remember the living

The Enemy on Both Sides

When the sun was born
the dark fell back into a mirror

the light went through exactly as far as it had come
so it was coming and going – or so it seemed

the sun looked in the mirror
he found he could see what he was thinking

first he thought only of himself
but that was too bright

he sighed and his breath caused smoke in the mirror
then in front of himself he saw a man

the man looked back in the mirror
between himself and the sun he saw woman

the woman looked back in the mirror
between herself and the man she saw child

the child looked back in the mirror
between himself and the woman he saw snake

the snake looked back in the mirror
but all he could see was the sun

but then he hesitated, for a moment
he fancied he too could see whatever he chose

for a moment he fancied he might see this or that
then the smoke cleared

the snake continued to look in the mirror
between himself and the sun he saw dark

so he curled up and went to sleep
it was finished. In the mirror dark faced itself.

Seed

There is rain falling by night
there is the thunder of water underground
there is steam rising in the sunlight

There is the seed inert in the dry earth
there is the seed stirring
there is growing towards the light, towards darkness

There is the dark earth
there is green earth at the new moon, at the full moon
there is earth growing yellow under the sun

There is earth
there is the seed
there is rain falling by night

There is the seed stirring
there is the thunder of water underground
there is the green earth

There is the seed growing
the steam rising
the earth turning yellow

There is the sun the moon and the earth
the man the woman and the child
there is the snake and the child and the tree

There is man and there is woman
there is a child and an old man

Finally there is the seed.

Corn

Corn
the cornbread
the plough

Corn
the cornbeer
the dance

Corn
the cornhusk
the grave

Three Dances

La Contradanza

We may not dance under the tree
unravel the coloured ribbons
and Tonantzin our mother has failed
then dance for the one with the stars in her hair
the newcomer
but by night before the new moon
secretly
we will sow.

Matachines
I black my face
and dance this way
frighten them with my squirrel-boy
I forget why
but the meaning is not lost on the living
when night comes
I will remember.

Pastoras
I will go back to the earth
I will leave my print frock
stockings of silk
shoes of patent leather
I will put on the *huipil* and dance
with crimson and blue
I will braid the darkness
All night I shall lie with the living.

Los Voladores

Four dancers are climbing the tree

the tallest in the wood
it has been fed blood
rooted in water
at the top is the star-eye
looking four ways

we are flying
we have become birds
our flight is to the earth

each circle more difficult to control
as the coil unwinds

the earth beneath is a mirror
four shadows hunt each other round and round
they believe they are free
but we are after them
they have only this much time

the four of us
thirteen complete turns
that is all the time there is
the rope played out
the eagle snatches the snake

now follows the earth-night
the end of the year
in the dark we dance
everything else forgotten
in joy, in stealth, in darkness

the snake-creature is climbing the tree.

The Noble Jaguar Will Continue to Die

El Maya chief of the hunters
the one with no father
he has killed him

they'll not see me weep
I'll dance for them
all day in the sun
that is enough

but if they could see behind the mask
they would know what has happened to my heart

the land is broken
by the sun
so is my heart
a deep arroyo in the dry season
I will sing their songs
but there is one song I will not sing

he is strong
can destroy seven farms in one night
seven villages
seven towns
he eats their tame cattle
can play cat and mouse even with the bull
carries away girls

but I and the other girls loved him
went with him willingly
in the forest he came when I called
I would lay his head blazing in my lap
because of that the she-dog was jealous
the one they call Wonder
she betrayed him
nosed him out
they led him into the square
called him cruel names
the sun blinded him
there in front of the church
they overpowered him
gave bits of him to the children to eat
they tore off his skin

tried it on for his strength
carried it away on a mule

I know where it lies
the sun eats the blood
but the skin is golden
gleaming

in the evening when the dancing is finished
I will fetch him back to the forest
he will stop with me all night
and in the morning when the sun comes
they will hear his roar
in the villages
the young girls will smile at one another
the rest will be afraid.

Saint Augustin Lorenzo

Still on the run, the outlaw

last week a boy with a kitten
no time at all they're the man and his horse
you hear them nights riding through
see nothing but the sparks fly

he has buried the silver in the mountains

Mardi Gras we gather
savages, Apaches, the Zapadores
all those whose worlds were ruined by creation

we welcome him with gunfire
crackers and dancing

a blanket of feathers

and he back to steal her away
to keep her safe
in hiding

for the time being they will live in the hills

at midnight we take off our masks
it is the time of darkness

the same each year.

The Yellow Flowers

The cradle – a circle of yellow flowers
my heart is beating – circled by yellow flowers
in loops round the drum – a circle of yellow flowers
in the sun the dancers – a circle of yellow flowers
above the open grave – a circle of yellow flowers
so are these words – a circle of yellow flowers.

The Day of the Dead

Morning
beyond the mountains
the sun has begun to drum
light floods the lake

we came here to sleep
sleeping we began to dream
dreaming we began to dance
into the night

toward morning the dark wore thin
the spell grew less certain
then the dance led us back
under the arch of flowers

now beside the grave
the bread remains
chillies and wine
the pumpkin untouched

or so it appears
but before we departed
before sunrise in fact
the living had eaten.

Cold Spell

1

Ice splinters
tinkle on the frozen slates
on the frozen trees
on the ice
ice tinkling on ice
the whole world tinkling
like a draft's moving strings of threaded shells
everything listens
it has begun to dawn on everything
that the ice is inventing silence
that this tinkle
is the beginning
of the end

2

The sun has passed too close to the sun
it has burned up
there is only an ember
molten ice cases the rocks
each pebble a clear saying
leaden cold
the sea is like something that has forgotten
why it is here.

Walking home
the valley already locked for the night
the way was scattered with birds
dying of cold
they scarcely troubled to hop
from under my boots.

3

All winter, not one poem.
Why the hurry?
The frozen moment was in store.

4

Dusk
her pony is lost
in the snow we follow the tracks
up through the oaktrees
out of the valley
we lose his trail in the lane
on top of the ridge where the ice is unprintable
in the dark
Stroller!
nothing listens
the world is too frozen cold
the stars are a fixed stare
there is nothing left to live for.

Tonight in meditation
my mind is clear as ice
and in the white surface
dusted with snow
this trail of clear hoof-prints.

5

Ice burns
after dark on the terrace
earth, stone and air are one black ice
standing still I am the eyes of the ice
open, dark, purely reflective
whatever I see is drilled into me
the point of a diamond
beneath a surface of ice
I am touched by the stars.

6

This afternoon they left
and I turned back from the snow-gleam
to the empty house
and the foot on the step
and the iron latch
and the door closing
and my feet across the tiled floor
played on the silence
the poem
that had been waiting.

7

The ivy, the yew and the cedar —
those three are the green.
Beneath the snow there are snowdrops
in perfect flower.

8

A chicken is clucking
that weak sound is the silence.

The sunlight is iceblue
the glare is the silence.
A blackbird in the gleaming snow
the blackbird is the silence.

9

The pony in the white field
meditating
he has let the thought go
the idea of grass.

10

Hawk-kill in the snow
a blackbird – the feathers scattered.
Had he picked one of the doves
I'd have seen only an open wound.

11

Coming back down the frozen valley
I heard my breathing
looked up and saw through the window of my hut
myself writing this poem

In my hut writing this poem
I was distracted by my breathing
looked up and out of the window saw myself
coming back down the frozen valley.

12

The sun is setting.
The silence in the sunlight
is opening itself
to the silence of dusk.

The two have met for the first time.
Now they wait for the silence of night.

13

Our bedroom empty
frozen sunlight falls on the bed
two pillows
we have filled the room with our sleep.
The light is afraid of waking us.

14

Over in the farm
Fred has managed to start the tractor.
The doves settle on the roof.
On the mat I threw out on the snow
the dog sleeps in the sun.
Sometime ago snow slid from the slates
a shadow passed the window.
The flock has broken up
the starlings come and go singly
black flakes of hunger.
I am listening, my mind not yet perfectly still.
On the surface the wind stirs a dust of snow.
Beneath there is the clear ice.
Soon I shall no longer hear the silence.

15

From our bedroom
I see the icicles under the fountain-bowl
have reached the frozen pool
the three are locked in meditation
it is difficult not to be drawn in

the telephone rings
I let it ring
we are so deep in silence
the phone is almost inaudible.

16

His footprints
returning across the white lawn
wander a circle
around the appletree.

And that is where he goes out
pulling the toboggan
running to the hill-field.

Today he is back at school.

17

My hand moves —
but for this thought
the frozen valley
brimmed with clear sunlight
would be completely still.

18

In the orchard the snow is broken —
a mole has unearthed
the earth.

19

Silence reflects in the water.
Silence reflects in the sound of the stream.
This evening the first birdsong in days —

a robin in the magnolia tree
is breaking the silence.

20

Night
I can hear the ice clenching on the slates
the house is locked in ice
and the stars can see themselves in the roof.

I close my eyes
and there is the sound of my breathing
the sound fills the silence exactly
the silence exactly fills the immense silent house
the silence, the dark, the breathing
and there is enough space
for everything.

21

Before the snow
the blackbird stopped singing
and became invisible.

When it had snowed
the doves on the roof had flown
but for their pink eyes.

Now the thaw –
I can barely detect where three magpies
have lighted in the wood.

22

A blackbird on the chimney,
two white doves on the roof-ridge –
the snow has begun to melt.

Wine Country

Away from the centre, the main street with the traffic, *les camions,* the Boulevard cafés – but not out of the town, not as far as the first detached houses, the yards with the guard dogs, or the derelict mill, the sluggish canal, green, bubbling with disuse, the road to the by-pass. The point is here, the stillness, as if the place had been overlooked, the appointment forgotten, or had become a backwater in the stream where time is measure by the cathedral bell.

I am expecting her, that she will come into the *Bar des Voyageurs.* I'll watch her leave the keys with the taciturn *patron.* Her face is alight. There is nothing between her and the moment. Nothing possesses her. She is going away for the night, or shopping, or to collect the children. I choose deliberately to sit here. I can hear the market, the cattle drone in the sunlight rung in brass. I breathe the clear, distilled light, and the morning bar-scent; and am so caught up in the stillness and the shadow of the market cries. I find the wine suddenly amber in the glass. I am alive to her. This is her vicinity.

It is always between two days: one of them is tomorrow, the other sometime in the past. Between what is certainly expected and the brilliance of what cannot be remembered for certain. That out of time feeling, the out of season, the feast day when the shops are shut and the pavements almost deserted – it's like a sudden winter memory of somewhere to the South, the moment between times, the siesta.

*

In the old town near the port, walking beneath the walls. Someone up on the third floor switches off the radio. The deserted place as it waits for the moment is listening to the pique of the sparrows around the puddle. There it is. The moment catches its breath. From behind the glass and lace of a bar door comes a scatter of bar laughter – somehow disembodied, a trick of time, as if the butt of its own joke. She is so close one feels that catch in one's throat. A little way down the street an unoiled slat-blind is being wound up, squeak by squeak, two syllables at a time, letting the day in slowly, and the light, and the silence. I wait, holding my breath because, although I can't quite remember, I am remembering the moment so exactly, this moment between moments. I glimpse her dark skirt beneath the blind. But then the blind squeaks on its way and the bent little woman in black is peering out. The scent of sun on stone walls, of wallflowers, gives way to the aroma of coffee.

*

Always away from the main thoroughfare. Here an old man is sitting under a lilac tree, beside his allotment, sorting his haricot beans. The train has stopped on the town embankment. He looks up unhurriedly. The silence and sun are alert. In the next compartment the older nun comments harshly, and the other, who is little more than a girl, is laughing. The world is full of worlds. At the foot of the embankment, not visible under the chest-nut tree, there is someone holding her breath. Or there's two of them not daring to breathe or to laugh. There's the two of us – until the train moves on, everything must live in suspense.

*

By the Loire, here is the moment. Under the wall of the chateau. A ledge in the sun. She is close. My mood is so full of her I am quite empty. The air is full of echoes, overbrims with her existence. *'Mignonne, allons voir si la Rose . . .'* The sun fills everything. Her name is on my lips. Cassandre. It is like the dove song filling the woods in our valley, or the moonless night scented with syringa filling our room. No space left for thought, the one air we breathe says it all. A single death-cry sounds in the chateau. Each moment the king is murdered. It is a moment we can retrieve. Love can stop the world any day.

*

But never in the full light. An *aperitif* in the shade in the Place Gordaine, or the first thought of siesta, or the Rue Bourbonnoux, *dans les ateliers* with the craftman slow time and light and colour of slow-seasoned wood. They are drawing the shutters, bringing down the blinds on the shops. The *épicerie* closes. I have missed her. She has slipped into the silence of the old town, the overhanging houses, slate-fronted, the drop-by-drop silence of craftsmen. Beyond the high stone wall I sense there's a garden – I can hear the silence, the trickle of water, the sound is cool, syrup-slow, coloured by the leaf shade.

*

O love I am home, I have come home demented. It is summer, our house, the visitors have just left, and the silence is coming back on tiptoe – behind us we hear it walking through the house. The two of us, and we are careful of the silence because

*we are a part of it, and the fountain, its liquid treble some-
where beyond the lupins, is a part of it, and the oaks breathing
in the heat. We look at each other across the silence and the
moment is laughing at us. Our own silent laughter has recognised
the moment. The silence smiles, is looking down at us from the
bedroom window.*

*

The shops have shut and the shutters are up. She is
unbelievably close, I can hear her beyond these shutters,
or those there on the first floor, in the cool deliberate
quiet, in the Bonnard-brown light, the table with the blue
and white china. She is this close – but for the wall I could
touch her. I think I did catch her scent.

*

Above the siesta the swifts fling round the chimneys.
Somewhere up in the Place George Sand, caught by
the moment a musician is playing a clarinet. I walk into the
shock-cool of the cathedral porch and hear the sound
behind caught in a tumbler, it rings far away, the colour is
purple, Phoenician, the song of the dove ... Oh Lady of
Bourges, I am in love wherever I look, wherever the
shadow falls, or the movement of her shadow catches
the corner of my eye.

*

When the children come out in the evening in the Place
Gordaine, when the air is love-warm with their calling,
and in the Rue Bourbonnoux *les ateliers* are silent, and
the air in the street smells of resin and linseed, and the
cathedral is silent, and somewhere in the purple half-light
up near the Place George Sand a musician is practising
the piano as though he's in love, as though in the pause
between phrases he's writing a letter, and the shutters are

coming down, squealing, a rattle, a clack, and there on the third floor, in the window overlooking the square, the dark silhouette of a girl, drying her hair. Who does not draw back. My heart is alert. She looks down on the darkening square, can see the figure standing by the fountain. Maybe she thinks for a moment it is him, the one for whom finally she'll loosen her hair.

*

My heart is aloud and I am in love. Can the dark conceal that I'm a fool's shadow passing, that I'm not really here. In the dark my love is alight. This whole scent I breathe is your breath. My real love is where I am. You are at home. Good night, when we are asleep I will continue to dream.

*

The shutters are thrown open in the Place Gordaine. In the last shadow-light a dove claps its wings. I breathe my way to the cathedral. After sleep the daylight is stretching thin and she may have gone to her mirror. Up ahead, at a second floor window, a hand with no ring is shaking a duster. Slow out of the sidestreets drifts the smell of roast coffee, the new smell of bread. Each day is a promise. The scent of roses. In a side-chapel an old woman puts pink roses on the altar of our Lady. Another day.

*

How did this France come suddenly by such beautiful children, such beautiful girls? She is so close I feel she might even venture out in full daylight. Is it laughter, a name whispered – it's like a hand through taffeta, this sound beyond the house of the Isére full of the Spring snow. Yes, she might make *le petit tour* in the Promenade. I am a boy in love, out of my depth in the town. Everywhere I look I find there is no contradiction. There is nothing else, nowhere else. When I meditate in Le Jardin de la Ville, under the vast plane trees, in the half-light of *chartreuse* and falling flowers, I am there. To be in love is to be a boy deranged in the afternoon. When the rest of the town sleeps its siesta. This afternoon so nearly she was there – a girl in *bureau de tourism* looking up from her writing to ask with her eyes, what was it I wanted? That grey light coming at me from far away, from a moment completely possessed. It could account for my life. Even the mountains with snow on them are distant. And this evening, drinking *kir* in Le Jardin de la Ville under the great plane trees, when the kids in the playground begin to fight, she's there again, belonging to no one but the moment, walking out from the crowd in the café, unaware how she has made a fool of the moment, caught it in the act, and the children too, catching their breath find their mood has changed.

*

At supper the graceful girl with the dark hair to her waist, fine to the bone, her grey eyes attentive, unaware how her sadness, hushed suddenly to a scent of violets. When at last she smiled the room brimmed with sadness, hushed suddenly to a scent of violets.

*

I have just woken. It is Sunday. Ah, here in the almost South in the town yet to stir, this, this could be her time. The traffic is still – one moped in the next street and, the sound surfacing from the silence, the fountains outside in the Rue Montorge.

*

They are the streams in our garden, the tinkle of the water at the end of the meadow. Am I awake? I am here. And when I ring I

find you with sleep in your eyes. Oh joy, you are happy. There is
sleep in your voice. I have no difficulty being here and now. Being
with you I do not wake from the present. I am in love for us both.
Wherever my eye falls it is she I am alive to. It is her I have
discovered. It is you at home in our bed.

*

It is raining. Slow summer rain. The air swims in the trees,
the earth is open and suddenly she is close. In the rain the
flowers are abandoned, the scent is on the air too heavy to
breathe, time can scarcely move. But when I put down the
phone I was lost. I'd mislaid the moment, had left it with
you. The line is cut. I am out of touch. Standing in the
Musée Dauphinois I remember winter. The words glimmer
through tears. I read you my letter. 'Il y a pas encore un moi
que tu as embarquer et il me semble qu' il y a des années sa me fait
tout oublier . . . il me semble qu'autor de moi que tout le monde
est plus heureux que nous . . . '

*

But then it was raining and the earth had come open, and
back after lunch to siesta in L'Auberge Napoleon, half-
asleep, listening to the fountain in the Place Grenette, I
hear again outside on the pavement the sound of her feet
and she goes by singing.

*

No, I have fallen from love. I am lost somewhere in
travelling, I have run down. The mountains are too close,
and too distant. I explore them minutely and cannot
discover anywhere for the two of us to be. The sun makes
no shadow, or where the clouds do make shadows on the
mountains that is too remote. Out of the train I can see
the stream, the trees in young leaf. I cannot understand
why there's no hint of her. Is this not the part between

seasons, lost within spring, between winter and summer, somewhere between the far North and the South, between southern noon and the beginning of the cool?

*

The heat is already less, it is getting towards evening. Everything is just so and not so, as she would have it. The smile or perhaps not the smile. The smile of La Giocanda. But she's *distraite,* has become totally vacant. The hour has slipped. The mountains are no longer the mountains. I cannot throw off the shadow. The girl in the train, or was it in the café, no it was the girl in the red skirt flying on her bicycle beside the blue lake in Annecy, stopping, one foot on the ground, her wrist on her black hair, her fingers on her forehead, to talk to the old man. She was alive, but she was nothing. I waited for her glance and she looked clean through me.

*

It is evening in Le Place St. Andréa, a meal before leaving on the night train. I can hear the sound of water, it must be the fountains or perhaps the cold Isère. Suddenly there is a scent like the scent of sandalwood. I look up – and I am looking at her. She has always been there, in her grey djellaba, the green band over her head, the Atlas-black eyes, *la sorcière.*

Yes, I hear it now, the sound of the snowflood in grey mountain river. A dream is settling the near side of dream. The water is cerulean in the sun. I am beginning to smile – I dare to smile now. She stands in the shade the far side of the river. And when she brings the salad Niçoise, the fish on the plate, I see her eyes have burned the secret bare.

I look on it and leave it intact. Later, on my way to the station, walking beside the cold flood-river. I think I

70

hear her calling. There, she comes running, breathless, one hand on her breast. I had left my book on the table. Her eyes are all laughter. This is the gift. The black eyes are so clear nothing is left but the clean gift of her leaving.

*

I am through being in love, this is love, I can feel the peace of it now. There is no shadow and almost no fear. Can this mean she has turned her back finally, that her scent, the swirl of her skirt will no longer inhabit the shadow, no further glimpse, in those times between seasons, in those times out of time, in those siesta moments when the town is hushed in the heat, the clink of a glass behind the shutters, the scent of varnish in the rue Bourbonnoux, the scent of basil oil from the empty salad bowl and where the plates have not yet been cleared from the table, the sigh from the room upstairs, the shadow at the window, the movement of the curtain?

*

I have taken the train through the upland, *le petit train jaune,* threading the meadows of the high Pyrenées, through the rare light where the gentians are jewels, Catalonia stretching away south, and catch the smell of the sky, am not looking now for anything exept to be here.

She is sitting across the way in the small compartment, holds her daughter to her as if to make room on the wooden seat. What do I know? I know this daughter is too like her father. The clear light of childhood is going from this child's eyes. She is becoming like her father, and her beautiful mother cannot do anything to prevent it. Madonna of the mountains and the snowline, you are so sad. You think your beauty is going unnoticed. From this moment beauty can never be lost. Your fingers, rough from the sink, grip the worn leather handbag as if you were threatened. The beautiful bones of your cheeks, sadness uses them to make a hollowness around your eyes, to make your cheeks hollow. But the lid is off the sky, the satin-grey sky opens in your eyes and the light is flooding from there. Between us is a shadow like the moment after the love-scream when all that possibility is slipping away and the mountains are closing in. You will not look at me. One foot in a girl's worn sandal moves ceaselessly, as if you are trying with your toe to write your name on the floor. The train stops. Even when I hand her down her shopping she will not look at me. She takes home a gift she won't ever accept.

*

Peace. Down from the mountains. My bedroom in the little Hotel de Terminus looks over the river. The melted snow, it is the flow of my sleep. A deep valley between the sky and the sea. Tonight it will come as no surprise if I break into the dream.

*

Tonight I dreamed. I was at home. You and I and our house were at peace. And unbelievably she was there too. Dazzling, petite, that beech-wood light, the sprinkle of it coming and going between the leaves. I had the feeling she had grown up a little, that she had come home like a difficult child, with the gift of her mischief. I could feel the two of them, her mischief and the old lunacy, set in our living room like two ornaments. But I was with you, quite at home. It was the two of us she was visiting. I wake at peace. I cannot break the thread of the river. It is before sunrise. I find a path up the mountain. The flowers, the thyme and broom and wild acacia, still in their night scent. I sit looking down on the stone village, Ville Franche where two snowfed rivers flow together with a sound like winter running away.

You are still asleep.

I sit on a stone and take my sandalwood beads from my pocket, begin to meditate. I find the sun has come over the mountain. I am meditating in sunlight. The world turns over. There is birdsong, the river way below like the sound in a shell – blackbird song between here and the river. Up on the mountain a cuckoo is calling in the sunlight. I can smell the flowers, the thyme, the seasoned earth – and now there is only the scent of sandalwood. The fragrance returns to the meditation.

*

In Le Jardin du Convent the old wind rustles the bamboos, chases the azalea petals. The Old Quimper is deserted. This town in the cold North has shut up shop. The shutters are up. They have all gone to sleep. The light is cold grey, it could be winter. I tiptoe down the Rue St. Nicolas, but she has gone. Below in the town the cold river is silent. The campers packing up, going back to the big city. The sun is worn thin. The wind fitful in the poplars, in the top of the eucalyptus. The voices clear from the swimming pool where only a few are left. The swimmers glance at the sun, they will not now get browner. The cars are ticking over, the roof-racks loaded. The girl in the blue bikini sits on her towel beside the pool, examining her feet. The sun does not touch her. Le Place Mesglonguen is empty. I sit for a time on the stone wall. Somewhere across the wind, a room on the first floor, a pianist is practising, Fauré, this same piercing phrase over and over. It is the moment, but I cannot feel that she is anywhere near.

*

I close my eyes. Everything is waiting. The sweetness has come so near to the surface. Sunlight, the sound of the river, the scent of the mountain thyme. There is only breathing this sweetness. So, love it isn't too difficult to smile now we are almost grown old. The warm wind speaks to the moment. I am here. We seem to have become immense. We are so vast that everyone, the entire world is playing around our knees like children. Our children. There is only the moment – and, when that has gone, the smell of sandalwood.

Songs

Deep within the Seed the Dream

Deep within the seed the dream
Half asleep I hear the rain
In what confine of the brain
Do I hear the falling rain
And know tomorrow's fields are green?

Deep within the dream the seed
Night is sighing sleep again
In what confine of the brain
Have I learned that winter rain
Annoints the summer in the seed?

Song

My father loved my mother with
Premeditated art;
At his given signal
They tore the earth apart.

But was it his to offer her,
And what was hers to take,

When I was comfortable asleep
Without the will to wake?

My father and my mother were
Cold-blooded man and wife;
They suffered with their one accord
My blind design on life.

Four Quarters

The wind has moved south
I don't recall when
I slept one moment
The garden turned green
The blackbird last evening
Sang it was spring
But this morning the cuckoo
And she has gone.

The wind has moved east
The year's growing old
I caught her whisper
The garden turned gold
The cuckoo last evening
Called summer in
But this morning the robin
And she has gone.

The wind has moved north
Its teeth are laid bare
I searched the garden
Found nobody there

The robin last evening
Cheeped autumn's song
But this morning the raven
And she has gone.

The wind has moved west
It shifted last night
I woke this morning
The garden was white
The raven last evening
Called winter home
But this morning the blackbird
And she was gone.

My Dream Is a Girl

My dream is a girl now spring has arrived
With rain and sun.
The hawk all winter tied in the snow
By a leather thong.
Tonight as I listen to the dreaming rain
I catch her song.

My way is a friend now summer is high
With sun and wind.
Throughout the short spring the hawk in the rain
Winged my mind.
Tonight I shall leave with the setting sun
My friend behind.

My song's an old man now autumn is here
With wind and snow.
All the long summer the hawk in the sun

Cast a shadow.
Tonight something moves about with the wind –
Taps my window.

My love is a child now winter has come
With snow and rain.
All autumn long the hawk in the wind
Cried in vain.
Tonight as I listen to the falling snow
He cries again.

Wendy's Song

Summerlong they glittered
The waves in Jenny's Cove
Their ring a silver warning
"You've been living on your love"
The white dazzle of her singing
Came fragmented like snow
"A paradise which only we
The young and proud may know."

Autumn from over Long Roost
He watched grey evening come
The breakers on the North Bank
Were blood in the setting sun
A raven down on the Devil's Slide
Croaked black as midnight snow
"That paradise which only we
The young and proud may know."

Midwinter on the Rattles
A voice from out of the grave

When summer lies in ruins
It will claim back all you saved
What heart will stop to remember
In a world too cold for snow
"The paradise which only we
The young and proud may know."

Come back again one April
Her name was gone from the stone
Went down to the Battery
In the hope I'd be alone
But up from the flowering ocean
A white petal storm of snow
"Here's paradise which only we
The young and proud may know."

Mai's Song

Sail away you lonely bird
What can you know of the sea
What can you know of the blue iceberg
That my heart has not coloured for me?

What do you know of the whale-road
Of the burning Arctic Sky
What can you see of the cold heartway
I've not seen with my innerward eye?

Sail away you lonely bird
Over the cavernous sea
There's nothing you'll find in the dark hidden deep
My heart cannot fathom for me.

Garden Path

The garden path, the window latch,
The strong virginia creeper –
Her breath, a scent; the hand, a touch –
We'd kissed, but then she's crying.
'Go slow,' she breathed, 'for what's begun
Will find a way of dying.'

The curtain lace, beneath the beam
A vase of crimson roses.
Our double bed, a broken dream.
Dear God, was that her crying?
"Be still," she said, "Whatever's born
Is a newborn way of dying."

The window cill, the unglazed pot,
White lily of the valley.
We hold our breath – from the wicker cot
Who on earth could this be crying?
'Don't move,' she said, 'it's the little one –
Our newborn love is dying.'

The summer dark, a nightingale,
The drift of orange blossom
A whisper tells the winter's tale –
'Now is the time for dying.'
'No wait!' she said, 'Oh can't you hear –
It's our newborn baby crying.'

Firewater &
The Miraculous Mandarin

An Event

To begin with, it is silent,
It could be night, or it could just be dark.
He feels he has arrived in a wilderness.

The earth is no longer safe,
The crust is moving in waves,
Is beginning to crack.
Something is about to happen:
The dark is no longer in doubt,
That dark is a prophecy that is beginning to dawn on itself.

Ah, there she is, the white moon –
The non-light sticking to the black violent sky.
This is the beginning.

The black is ready to burst.
The black wind is coming
Out of the horrible mouth of the moon.

The wind has already reached the earth;
It is somewhere behind, somewhere in the wood.
The earth is prepared to respond with violence.

The wood is being taken over.
Someone back there is trying not to scream.
He can feel that scream in his throat – it sticks like a label.

The wind is leaving the wood.
It is coming, it opens the curtains –
It will obliterate everything in the house.

Wait! Somewhere under his feet is the sound of water –
This must be the stream.
The sound is like going back to before the beginning.

The wind thrashes past him;
The scream thrusts its hands over his ears –
So tight he can no longer hear it.

And he can no longer see the light properly;
It has become a blank face staring over his shoulder
Into the face of the wind.

And the face is becoming black.
It has been impressed by the wind,
Is becoming an angel with a black face.

The angel is trying to fasten its mouth over his mouth,
The black breath – he is being smothered in it.
Any moment now everything will have gone black.

The angel is beginning to smile.
It crams his mouth with its black tongue.
The light is going out.

He thinks he can feel a stabbing pain.
He thinks maybe it's his fear coming to a point.
There! the scream again, screaming out of a nick in his thigh.

And the light is opening between his eyes
And under the bridge there is still the water
And perhaps another sound like the sound of voices.

He opens his eyes.
It is night.
The sky is opening out towards the stars.

The air is still, it is windless.
Something settles on his lips – it is like a label.
It is the name that has always been on the tip of his tongue.

The light continues to open outwards –
Beyond it there is light opening
Like the door at the head of the stairs.

He finds he can see past the light
To the light.
He finds he can see all the way.

Changeling

He shivers at the sound of the wind
I hold him

He thinks he's in the hulk of a liner, he thinks there's a storm

This neck round his neck has been drawn too tight
I hold him

He wants none of it

He squeals – he can't take this beating
I hold him

His father might find him, he trembles

He is in danger of coming in two
I hold him

He is possessed

He is giving birth, screaming
I hold him

He has mothered an imp

He has fallen into a deep sleep
I hold him

He is terrified by the baboon's laughter

He shakes, he is afraid of his own strength
I hold him

He wants desperately to stand on his own two feet

He cannot let go
I hold him

He is determined to do himself an injury

Someone has let him loose with a knife
I hold him

None of us is safe – she least of all

He screams – and then he screams
I hold him

He wakes with a start

He has seen me, he is opening his arms
I hold him

I am holding him.

The Way Through

The baby won't stop crying. This casts a shadow over
  everything.
The devil would love to stop laughing. The laughter's
  killing him,

The baby is in love with his miserable image of himself.
The devil roars with laughter. No one can hear. It drives
  him crazy.

The baby feels his misery is coming along nicely.
The devil laughs. He can match anything for size.

The baby wants his mummy all to himself.
The devil has had mummy. He stuck a knife in her back.

The baby feels guilty. He enjoys every moment of it.
The devil suspects he's in the clear. The thought makes
  him uneasy.

The baby thinks he should hide in the cupboard.
The devil is with him all the way.

This time the baby won't come out until he's ready.
The devil's not sure he's prepared to wait that long.

The baby thinks he hears his dad coming.
'Cave,' says the devil. 'Here comes God.'

There's wind outside. It cuffs the house.
It cuts clean through the building.

The baby opens his eyes. The room is full of light.
The devil lies on his back on the carpet and roars.

The baby has seen the devil.
The devil has stopped laughing.

The baby smiles. He's had an idea.
The devil feels uncomfortable. But can't see any other way out.

The baby is getting sleepy.
The devil is appalled. The waters are beginning to break.

The baby is asleep.
The devil is in labour.

Opus

> The *imaginatio,* as the alchemists understand it, is in truth a key that opens the door to the secret of the *opus* . . . The place or medium of realisation is neither mind nor matter, but the intermediate realm of subtle reality which can be adequately expressed only by symbol. The symbol is neither abstract nor concrete, neither rational nor irrational, neither real nor unreal. It is always both.
>
> C. G. Jung, *Psychology and Alchemy*

The house is dark
I am not sure what I am
I'm not sure how this will turn out
Everything is possible

1

A curious wind
Is coming from under the floor
Too hot and too rough
Everything it touches needs to tremb.e
And quite empty
Like a wind turned inside out
Except for its belly
Which is like a stone
Which is full of fire
Which is full of blue water
Which is full of a filmy shadow
Which has yet to make up its mind

2

The hearth
A blue fourstone
Like the still of a river
If it moved it would be transparent
Frozen it conceals everything
Two firedogs loom like water towers
Two grey giants
Everything is on top of them
They have been given no choice
They have nothing to look forward to

3

The spent ash is beginning to dither
Like a tray of pins tapped with a finger
The wind is milking it
The dead coals begin to glow

Something is wriggling into life
Shakes a whisper of grey moondust from its back
Attacks the air
It has leathery wings
Four fiery heads
The whole thing is coming on heat

4

The water in the glass is innocent
The heat fills it everywhere like pain
It chatters on the hob
The floor of the bowl bubbles
Light from four points
Collides in the centre
A rash of colour
A laser phantom
A transfiguration
That would float straight to the surface
Except it's tied to two repulsive animals
Except it's at the end of its tether

5

The heat is stacked in the chimney
The sleeper's lungs are powdery with soot
He dreams the way a stone dreams
With no movement of the eyes
Something he could never imagine
A trap through the sky

6

The water a cloud
Inert as a junket

But the icy wind
Brings it out in a muck sweat
Curdles it like bad blood
Clots it like milk
The whole pail gone off
The father and mother of a mess
The pit of the stomach
Sweet as a tanner's van
The offal shop
The loom
The solar plexus

7

Ravens wriggling out of the black sea
Croaking off through the smoke
With no hope of land
Until this fluke
This rock, this hillock
This enlargement
This mountain shining like darkened liver
In a drench of sweat –
The real heart of the matter
With a topping of snow

8

The wind has blown up an unaccountable treat
Drawn off a rank of cloud from the gungy sea
Clean electric rain
A power line
Running back down the mountain in a silver stream
Enough to melt the heart

9

In the attic the lovers have woken
They can't think how they come to be here
Where the heart of the fire is everywhere
They can't think how they come to be beautiful
They picture each other across a silver sea
Two dark continents
They can't think how they come to be black

10

The sun loses itself in the moon's shadow
The moon is lost in the shadow of the earth
The earth has sunk without trace under the sea

11

The swan is a white shuttle
The swan breathes through the eyes of the wind
The wind doesn't shadow the sky
Or chalk the sea
The swan may not even be there
So that whatever he comes between
Like the sun and the moon
Or the lovers themselves
Are no longer apart

The swan is the white shuttle
The mirror
In which space conceives
The illusion of space

12

A fiery cool breath
Burns up through the floor of the head

Pale and blue as a cloud
We are prepared to drown in it
No thought rides on the surface
I am dragged under
My eyes are out
This silver sea will run everything together
We are forgetting one another

13

What happened then was like waking
The sea had washed everything away
The substance of this circle is single
Fire
But not fire
But not water
But not gold
But equally not silver
No less hers than his

14

Beyond that only the chill fire
The silence that answers the swan's cry
It is the cry of the phoenix

The house is on fire
I am in smithereens
I am this dust of sparks
Flying like silver birds
Fixed like a gas of golden stars
In the face of this brilliant night

Firewater

You are like water
A dew-lake
Or a blue meadow
A mist of blue flax
Cornflowers in a meadow of oats

I have dug a deep well
I have struck shillet
I am on fire
I cannot live with myself

You are a rivulet
A ripple breaking on a dark shoreline
I am like a boy
A prince left behind in the afternoon
I have wandered through the empty rooms
Have found my way into the Queen's apartment
Have discovered her wardrobe
And hide in the dark
Feel the blue silk against my cheek
It is liquid
The cool satin
Purple and deep green
I breathe her scent
And the joy of it is like a pain everywhere
I am coming alive

You are uncommonly patient
Nothing can distract you
Your concentration is complete
When you are perfectly still

Then everything is moving
You are wide open
This pinpoint of light
In you it is everywhere
I see it wherever I look

You are like the sea at first light
A pitcher of white gold
In the V of the valley
You are like the bead of water in the lup_n leaf
Or like the whole ocean
You are like a riddle
To which the answer is a riddle
To which you are the answer

What is it of me that moves in you?
I am programmed to burn up
What is it about me you respond to?
You have no idea
You have been taken entirely by surprise
You have given yourself away

When I look at you
I catch my breath
When our eyes meet
I feel I might not breathe ever again

You are like midday
Or else a cloudless evening
A blue sky that is mirroring the sea
That mirrors the sky
When you close your eyes
You become unknown

Like a soul in suspense
In the silence between two breaths
Between two heartbeats
Between mantra and mantra
The fire and the fire

My longing is inexpressible
It is as if I must hold my breath
At the same moment as I breathe your name
As if I were seeing you reflected in my own eyes
As if my excitement were drawing joy
From the pain of our being apart
As if in the green shadow beneath the lime trees
Were the laughter of full sunlight

Like a waterfall in a wood you radiate cold
Your openness accounts for everything
It is irresistible
Everything is enamoured
Flame is drawn to it
Barely touches the surface with its tongue
And the skin sticks
It might be frozen to steel
The surface burns like ice
The skin of the flame is melted
And the fire has run out

Flame is running like water
It is into everything

It has coloured the water sun-red
The whole pitcher is inflamed
The centre is burned out

I don't think I can go on
I am awash with fire

And the air is fire-water
An eau-de-vie
It is pure spirit
I am frightened to breathe

The heart of the fire is gone out
The walls of the kiln will crumble
Water will be into the gallery
It is finding its level
It is becoming like air
No, on the lips it is like milk
With the flavour of fire
I drink
I heard a sound like a sigh
The ceiling is open
It has become a cloud of blue light
A vapour
A breath of smoke

We can breathe again
We can hold our breath

And the blue light over our bed
And in the evening the scent of lime flowers
And the sound of the fountain
And the green woodpecker on the trunk of the medlar
And when the air moves
The tinkle of a string of shells
And from the shadow beside the bamboos
A single blackbird
His song reduced to light

This moment is here
It is where we touch

And the warm night wind on my cheek
Or your cheek or you hair or your breath

Your eyes have opened my eyes
The light is on fire
It is air it is breath
I breathe your breath
Your breath is like blue milk
It is on fire
Your eyes are awash with light
I can see no end to it
I have no more to say.

Song

A heartbreak song the life in my vein
    A baby locked in stone
But I will steal in the deepest mine
    Rubies from the moon

But I will steal in the deepest mine
    Rubies locked in stone
A heartbreak song the life in my vein
    A baby from the moon

Genesis

God was lost in meditation
His own name was the mantra
There could be no distraction

But then God had another idea
If he chose he could become aware of his own breathing
He took a deep breath – everything came alight
He let the breath go – everything became dark
In their own way the light and the dark were equally good

He took another breath, his second
This time the idea was like a bubble, completely round
Probably it was microscopic, though it seemed enormous
Either way there was nothing one could add
It fitted him completely
God felt excited – this was good

For a moment he thought his third breath had been a mistake
The bubble had burst, the whole thing was getting out of hand
It was like a greenhouse,
It was beginning to run riot
Then God saw that he'd had another idea
Everything had suddenly come into flower
Next moment there were seeds everywhere
Each one complete, each one a little bubble
God saw the joke
He laughed, a good belly-laugh
The joke had been at his expense

The next breath was painful
There was still the bubble
But it was beginning to come in two

He must have had the idea that it should be red
Because the pain – it was enough to break one's heart
But when he breathed out, that was the first sigh of content
He felt at home
What had appeared a bad idea was turning out for the best

God took a fifth breath
It occurred to him maybe he was a monkey
This idea stuck in his gullet
He realised he could as easily choose to be a bird
Or a fish
But no, it was this monkey idea that insisted on taking shape
Now when he breathed, the air whistled down inside him
Where it became water fire stone and blood
It was the source of intense excitement
The possibility of getting on in the world
But also of slipping back into a bubble
Or of escaping into chaos
God had no option but to take another breath

The sixth breath – the light hit him between the eyes
It almost blinded him
It was as if he had held up a mirror to his own light
As if his whole experience had assumed a single form
There was the light and the shadow
There was the bubble
And the garden getting out of hand
And the heart come in two
And everything in the balance of one breath
All this in a single figure
As if his *I am* mantra had been translated into form
Soahum, he heard himself say
And with that the image of the man –

Or was it a woman? –
Began to come apart in the light
I am that – God repeated the mantra
The figure had almost disappeared
It had been perfect, the image of himself
It had after all been an excellent idea
– *that I am,* he concluded

Somehow his own name had acquired a new meaning.

God took one last breath
It was complete
Once again he was lost in meditation
Now there would be no further distraction.

Mooney's Sin

Mooney toeing his lonely line
Encounters three colourful men
Each one humping a travelling pack,
Mooney a ball-point pen.

Those three have their heads in the air
Keeping tabs on a tell-tale star;
Mooney is dazed by the sky herself –
Revealing, blue, demure.

Those three are drawn by Herod the king –
He rules them out of court;
While Mooney recites his twice times two
The others wonder what to do
When 'Shalt not' collides with 'Ought'.

Flush out of ideas beside the sea
The three try to snatch some sleep,
But Mooney retrieves their headlong star
From the blue skirt of the deep.

A stable on the edge of town,
This child with a gleaming grin –
While the three wise men unpack their bags
Mooney commits his sin.

While the three wise men uncover their store
Mooney's heart has sung to a stop –
The child is fine but, heavens above,
This girl with a gift of a lap!

The first unwraps his bar of gold –
The child puts the crown on his head;
Mooney finds he's lost for words,
Smiles at the lady instead.

The second makes much of his pungent stuff
That fills the air like pot-pourri;
Mooney sniffs the cornflower scent
Of this girl the others don't see.

The third has come up with a dreadful thing –
It smells like birth, or the grave;
Mooney lost in her wonderful smile
Has forgotten how to behave.

Round he turns on the three wise men.
Then horror! He's down on his knee –
Father, Holy Ghost and Son,
The awful Trinity!

'Father, Holy Ghost and Son
Your gifts to your smiling boy!
But the awkward gift of my little song
Belongs to the Mother of Joy.

Blue, blue heaven that carries the sun
Withdrawn in the blue above,
Or blue under blue, the reflective deep,
Womb to the stars of dreaming sleep,
Mia Donna and Mother of Love.'

Milarepa and the Five Wisdoms

1 Vajra

His anger mounts
The snow has become a fixed glare

When he tries to breathe
A white sheet is drawn over his mouth

The mountains lean on him
The world closes in

His whole territory has shrunk
To the confine of his head

There is no distinction
Between himself and his blind anger

The world has crowded him out
And now everything is a threat

    Milarepa managed a sigh
    Mountain after mountain slipped back

And it was clearly morning

Cold light on the eastern brim

Winter – the ice in needles
Glittering from the roof

The light spread like clean water
Feeling its way over everything

A mirror in which the eye sees in each detail
The image of itself

And his mind is extended to cover everything
So everything has room to move

And room to breathe
Without crowding Milarepa

2 Ratna

All in a breath
And this simple achievement takes his breath away

Look at the gold garden – an unbelievable crop
His satisfaction is a positive danger

So crimson ripe it could split like a fruit
And the black pips – they'd then be everywhere

Even the surrounding stone wall is accomplished
Outside is a world apart

Nothing more to be done – the bees are bored
The ripest pear going soft from the centre

He has completed the house – and the garden
Milarepa realises with a sense of failure

> Milarepa gave up on the riddle – he had seen the answer
> That the answer could never come up with the answer

So the thought of being breathless – he shrugged it off

His lungs were full of air

The tip of his finger on the amber earth
He found he had drawn a perfect circle

He let go of the need to let go
Sunlight was already filling his head

He pictured the wall fallen – a grey rubble
Riddled with peacocks and red admirals

When he smiled the intruders walked away
As if he had ceased to exist

Standing in the completed porch he thought
This might be the perfect place to build my house

3 *Padma*

A foxy scent has rushed him off his feet
He's flush with it

Yes this is him – this syrupy oblivion
All he now needs is to be out of his mind

Past that painted face
Painted on the face of his panic

There's room for nobody else
Not if one's to lose oneself completely

If only it were possible to have had her already
Right down to the quick blackout

The business over and done with
Swallowed whole – beginning with his tongue

    It happened – in his mind everything was wiped out
    Milarepa found himself with breathing space

His breath was so slow he might have forgotten

And she was what was left of the sun – a warm stain

His breathing imperceptible
But the milky flavour gave her away – she was the breath

He thought himself wide open – his lungs were alight
And she overbrimmed she was the scent of bluebells

Another breath
And she showed up in the flowering oak

The open upland settled to the spring night
He stopped breathing – his lungs continued to fill

He breathed out slowly – this time she remained
Milarepa abandoned himself

4 Karma

A hailstorm
Has everything springing to life

The white earth begins to come apart
Uncovering a brilliant plot

Now the south wind will never let up –
Heat is thrusting the air like a glove

Grass-seed nettles his skin, pollen his eyes
The cuckoo flies cuckooing into his head

And all the time nextdoor is achieving the impossible
Not a weed between the rows

He listens. The plot is thickening
And somewhere under it all lies his original patch

> Milarepa choked – he wiped his eyes
> The garden stretched to infinity

Evening – shadow had stepped out from the shadows
The green earth had grown together

A white moth collided with the wood
The trees woke quivering

Hookweed hooked the horizon
Drew everything closer

He moved – his foot spilled a lily
In all events he was indispensable

So he gave up and closed his eyes
The dark was neat with a thousand fragrances

When the air is perfectly still, he thought
The four winds are all blowing at once

5 Buddha

Milarepa is beginning to see through everything
Now in winter he hoards his boredom indoors

In spring he can glimpse beneath the glamour
When she walks out of the door she leaves him untouched

In summer he barely registers the fever
As he stands to applaud the bare earth

In autumn with so much wine spilt
Even to get drunk is too much trouble

There remains only himself for company
But these two don't get on so well any more

Boredom is to blame
Inactivity itself is wearing thin

> Milarepa yawned
> Until the black behind his eyes began to scramble

He saw the world turn back to front
Boredom was being torn in two

He saw he was about to quit
He would watch himself walk out of the house

And leave nothing behind – except emptiness
Which was already attaching itself to the memory of itself

He despaired. And it was like being struck with a slipper
He opened all his eyes

Emptiness was filling his emptiness to the brim
There was room for everything – for a hundred thousand
songs

When nothing is left, he thought
The first star brings everything to light

Life Story

My father died and left
My mother all to me;
I took her at face value
And that left father free.

Under her loving gaze
I bore my father's stamp
A thing she thought she'd have –
I fixed her in the grave.

So mother's off back to dad,
A manly give and take,
Till being both dead and gone
They both climb on my back.

So then I dug them up
And patched their eyes with stars.
  I've packed them off to bed –
  While I grow up instead.

The Seventh Wave

The first wave broke
Midnight turned over
The curtain moved

The second time
Under the hawthorn
A blackbird sang

Third, a mistake
A single white rose
Her scent missing

Broken in two
The heart is mirrored –
Forms the fourth piece

The fifth last pain
There on your clean sheet
Blood – and water

Her dark sixth sense
A sudden fragrance
Of black jasmine

The seventh wave
All seven flavours
Of the apple.

Three Promises

Between the sheets of midnight and morning
A dream

At first light there's frost
Fields of white manna

In sunlight moment by moment
The day stretches out

A dream, manna, this moment
Three promises you'll never keep.

Song before Birth

What should I see the house go broke
You swallow it down you swallow it down

What if a shadow as big as a room
You open your arms you gather it home

What should I hear my mother's scream
Open your ears open your eyes

What if a girl and her dress in flame
You open your arms you gather her in

What should you hear her scream again
Open your eyes take a deep breath

What if a dog a wolf or a tiger
Open your throat loosen his collar

What should the idiot jump on my back
Carry him home open your door

What if he stow his boot on my neck
Undo the laces wipe his feet

What should a girl and her dress be red
Open your heart take the knife

What if I see my father come
You gather him in you swallow him down

What should a girl and her dress be green
Take a deep breath swallow the rain

What if the lightning what if thunder
Open your eyes your heart your mind

What should a girl and her dress be blue
Give yourself up drink her down

What if a girl and her dress is snow
Drink her down swallow her breath

What should a girl and her dress be black
Roll up the sky uncover the night

What if her eyes be blank as skulls
Open your arms gather her home

What should I darken the face of God
Unlock your skull let him in

What if the sea the sun or stars
Swallow it down swallow it down

What should I see the world go broke
Swallow it down you swallow it down

And what if that horror that feeds on horror
Breathe on the glass wipe the mirror

From
Practice

a travel sequence

Difficult day, hours piling up
　　Like unpaid bills. Morning yawns
At the back of it. Evening
　　Hoards the lack of achievement.

Meditation achieves nothing.
　　Nothing dawns – out of nothing.
Lamplight on the window blacks out
　　The world. This black achieves black.
　　　　　　*

Wind, a deep breath up from the sea.
　　Toiling by's a blue-bottle
On the trail of somebody's death.
　　He planes into the window.

Picks himself up and labours off
　　On full-throttle. So once more
It seems the universe survived.
　　The wind dies. I breathe again.
　　　　　　*

A bee blazes past the window.
　　I've been stung – taste on my lips
Stolen honey. How many bees
　　I wonder, how many flowers

Lost in that one flavour? Millions.
  Those bee-trips back to the hive!
The thief won't let go. That old sting
  Maddens the bees like thunder.

              *

Too distracted to meditate
  The trees hold their breath, thinking
How the leaves can't begin to fall
  Till they let go. I let go.

'Hear with your eyes,' Dongshan says.
  I see nothing, not one breath . . .
Just a sudden shower of gold leaf,
  The stream beginning to flow.

              *

High over Santiago gulls
  Drift down the evening home
To some Gull Rock — and I'm watching
  As twilight brims our valley.

Beside the Rio Lima I sit
  And am at home listening
To the valley as blackbird song
  Dims the October twilight.

              *

PONTE DA BARCA

Fish keeps two days. I feel the road's,
  The vagrant's call to nowhere,
Yesterday's sun; today no wind,
  The river flowing backwards.

I know the way home is *today,*
  But this two day's here's grown stale.

I'm drawn South. The river repeats.
  A smell of fish. The road knows.

                    *

Always I am awake and she
  Is the one who is dreaming,
Her head on my chest, me alive
  To the rise and fall of hers.

I'm awake; she's the one dreaming —
  I watching the sky above
Iguacu; she dreaming deep
  About a vast waterfall.

                    *

SATORI AT IGUACU

'Mightier than the thunder of
  Many waters . . . ' O God O
Iguacu. Always this sound
  At the back of sound. Water.

Behind thunder always the still
  Of her name. O that water.
Midnight the waters dreamed her face.
  Her face at midnight is black.

                    *

Still further south — the cryptic stars
  Are distinct ice, the near-dark
Smells antarctic, cold sun has fused
  The live volcano. And down

The grey shoreline four ghostbirds come
  Tipping the swell with immense
Slow wingbeats, south to the snowfires
  Of Tierra del Fuego.

                    *

NORTH CANTERBURY

The squeal-scrape of the barrow's wheel,
And yet this morning's magpie
Song's oiled sweet as a carousel.
  The air is hay, and the sheep

Stammer's clarion webbing
  Stitched under the sky, stretching
The ochre plains out to mindless
  Blue, mountains as clear as day.

*

WAITATI

Only this room, and I've arrived,
  Still the smell on me of dark −
The darkness. The curtain stirs and
  I'm aware of her, the glare

Of her absence, and of the glare.
  Outside the larks singing. Then
The bellbird. *Waitati*. Summer's
  Soft touch. A touch of winter.

*

WANAKA

Waking, and she beside me cried
  In her sleep. Come straight from dream:
Goodbye to an old friend. God, how
  The half-light clings. Kaa! I 'raise

My voice to silence the echo'.
  That catches the gleam: ringing
In the corridors of the trees
  A blackbird had sung. Sang. Sings.

*

TIMARU

A gym-slip in the front row, she
  The most present, most aware,
My mother, as if she'd glimpsed this
  Stillborn me a lifetime on

Perusing her – the son she'd cast
  On her raft of hair to sea,
Come home at last to where she lives
  Still in the manapau trees.

*

COOK STRAIT – LEAVING SOUTH ISLAND

Always leaving by sea. The land
  Goes down in mist. One mountain
To the East, the snow summit clear
  Above the haze. There's something

Acquisitive about leaving –
  I'm left counting memories
Of her I'd only invented.
  The glare softens to her gaze.

*

BESIDE THE MURRAY

Clogged. Pulmonary vein . . . of mud.
  Hear it? The slow pulse of slop
In the cellar, the living-room,
  Blood-thick, a flood of grey paste:

Crumbling water. Fish taste of mud,
  Grey dollops of mud, that plop
Into the silt air while red gums
  Make a meal of it, of mud.

*

In a blue sarong he tiptoes
  Barefoot past our door. He sweeps
The path. His sister bows, filling
  A plate with sweets for the gods.

Meanwhile behind me on our bed
  She sleeps. I write – emptiness
Into mind. The South wind's brought rain
  Two warships pass in the strait.

                    *

Silence – like the first shock of ice,
  Like a drink from the ice-spring,
The last resort, and I've so much
  Need to come home to silence

I'm hearing snow, the stain of it,
  Snow lagging the silence –
Someone on tiptoe who drifts
  Between myself and the stream.

Uncollected Poems & Songs

Water Scales

I keep coming back to water.

The Mardle, the stream's name, the way the water sounded.
In winter a child's river.

In summer up to my ankles, twenty steps down from the
waterfall, running broad like a mill-pool in the wind, or a
pond of whoppers. Conferring beneath the bridge, under
the arch, a sheet of corrugated sound, the garden's limit.

It was this water my father bought the mill for, fished it
three leaves before, called once again to the front, he went
overseas. A last time.

My life was then (is still) towards the stream.

Summers down a flag-path past beds of columbine and
phlox to the stream's bank, could swim or swing on a rope
over the deepest pool. Could drown in winter.

Now back from school my footsteps are my kids' as
they run with the hill pulling away like a mat under their
feet, down into the valley, inch an eye over the bridge's
parapet. Strawberry Water; that is their stream.

The half-pound trout, still in sunlight like an opal brooch, all-eyes, just the blade of his tail feathering.

Lying awake a child would hear in the strands of sound the stream's name. Mardle. Only the ear tuned by winter, a still day with the stream in spate in a valley of phantom oaks, filling the valley with its grey clangour, can catch any hour of the year the stream's temper – call it galvanized, a foundry finish, anvil and hammer.

But catch it once and even the summer drought will ring. Listen. You'll fancy you hear the gnat's wings on the little pools, clear as god's-eyes, ping like a dry kettle, and the trickle under the stones, from deep in the throat, the clink of coins in a bottle, still metallic.

My beat upstream was three fields. That way the world was a labyrinth under the bracken, voices for company, in and out of the woods. Never alone beyond the point one saw the moors. It wasn't the earth their view uncovered but the sky, and something else unthinkable . . . One day.

I found the stream's source in a tor-side hollow, blank except for a bird's shadow. Out of rancid peat, red-oxide and bull's blood, the water sprang. Saw the hill spread-eagled, the water spurt from Christ's side. This wound at the core.

Entirely another mood would choose downstream. An exploration not so much of end as circumstance.

Two meadows, a long orchard, and there silent as the mystery ship the farm preoccupied and unattended – the cows burping in the shippon, moody to be milked, the smell of baking, out front the table laid under the monkey-

Your arms fallen either side of his neck
Your face in his mane –
Browsing the banks, grazing sleep

The ten years you grew from that girl
We drawing the curtains first thing
Would see him down the valley
Among the heifers, scrunching the dew
Beginning to steam

Discovered at last after the donkey died
There's a pain called *being lonely* –
That the ageless too can grow old

That moment the meadows and woods of his world
Became unbridled
No feeling for the needle
Only the sweetness of your fingers
And the sugared bran
Until that too emptied from his mind
The blue sky became mist in his eye and he –

In the still woods all around
Such a shower of gold leaves –

Falls on the silence.

Jack

In that summer's gloaming
On his way from the farm
To None-go-by Cottage
Turned to my car

And I saw for a moment
The mid-summer sky
That warmth and that glare
Cold clearness of ice
The flint of the loner.

Saw him in that twilight
Take the pipe from his mouth
Spit a slow loop
Then start to speak
Gold words back of time
Of unbelievable harvest
Of hives overflowing
The nights making music
The storm and the shipwreck
That built None-go-by.

And the memory stayed
A vision to stand
For ever under Embury
How the eye by its witness
Can make love of a wildness
Make even of its loneliness
Of even its passing
The sole undersigning
At the foot of a globe
Of beholden beauty.

And now mid-winter
I feel he has gone
In the night from his valley
Can feel it without him
Can feel an aloneness

And silent the morning
Round None-go-by Cottage
Where the white fetch of winter
At the third call of ice
Has stamped its silence.

The Faggot

The fig, our nakedness before the fire.
Blackthorn, the spite – a thin smoke.
Oak, the heartwood.
Ash, a staff.
Beech, like a stone in two.
Yew, a sustainable sorrow.
The reed, answer to the storm.
O cedar – O my Lebanon!
Ivy, the green in winter.
Willow, the wand in the rune.
Holly, a birth – the spark in the fire.
Juniper, the fragrance.
Sycamore, a brittle rung.
Briar – anger anger anger.
The blood of the one who binds the faggot.
Viburnum, the flower of winter.
I bid them all burn –
Oh, and a wild rose –
A happy New Year.

Le Cosquer

'Ce Muscadet est surnommé "Fringant" parceque
plein de jeunesse et ombrageux comme un pur sang.
Preuve de sa vitalité, il se trouble quelquefois et perle
aux changements de lune et quand la vigne est en
fleur, ou aux vendages . . . mais aussi sans raison, par
manière de fantasie!'

From the label on a bottle of Muscadet sur Lie

I

The Muscadet has cleared. The morning air
That carried from first light a cutting edge
Now softens down to the warm body of the vine.
My wife is home.
Spring sunlight, after Le Cosquer,
Is the still of wine.

This valley is a liquid thoroughfare,
Green liquor-vat of scented Armourique,
Its drift mere inference. It is a watermead
Where, shadowfree,
White flints gleam and disappear
To a drifting weed.

The soma flows. About my hut each green layer
Of terraced leaf dips to this mindless strain.
A firecrest pheasant calls: the cry flutters, like a moth
In Green Chartreuse.
Two bees, drenched, whine through the air;
Syrup drowns them both.

Sopping in one tied corner of the glare
A spider rings a rhinestone universe.
The grass is luscious. Across the valley the cows
Tread deep water:
They're new-washed china. Drunk, they stare —
They miss their shadows.

Now she comes into vision, walking where
Her long skirt draws a dark trail in the dew.
Below my hut she kneels. One seed has cracked the earth.
She pulls a weed.
Then stops — listening, half-unaware,
To the strain of death.

Our valley brims. The Muscadet is clear.
I gather in the meaning of the wine.
The world stops. The valley's a cup whose lip is sealed.
No shadows move.
The shadow world, save Le Cosquer,
Is beyond our field.

2

The wind picks up; the day slips into gear.
The shadows find their focus in the grass.
The skeins of quiet regather where my gold is pinned.
She moves her head:
Magic spinning from her hair
On the liquid wind.

Where has she been to fetch her eyes so clear?
Could the vision have broken from my head?
Or was it she who went, I who was left alone?

Perhaps the chill
That I contracted there
Has followed me home.

Sometimes I'll pray, if she'll contain the prayer.
I'll find her home, the garden and the house.
So she is light: so must I double bed with death
Whose shadow shows
Only when she does not dare
To inhale his breath.

She starts, as if she shied away from fear,
As if this strain had caught her by surprise.
She looks down. One hand flicks a spider from her blouse.
And then she smiles,
And with the shade of Le Cosquer
Walks towards the house.

Beneath our roof we'll keep this empty chair,
And set it at the table when we eat.
He shall be welcome. When the loving-cup is passed
His vacant breath
Falling cold on the earth's bare
Lip shall be our last.

So now midday. The Muscadet is clear.
Shadow has shortened to the point of noon.
Warmth has uncovered the full body of the vine.
My wife is home.
Spring sunlight after Le Cosquer
Is the still of wine.

Fallen Star

Love-cry in the heart of grief
Behind the mask a young girl's face
Whose tears in front of her smile?
What blood behind the white lace?

His bayonet has slit the seam
A child jumps out unharmed
The cold glare comes down to his gaze
A terrorist world disarmed.

A dolphin dead on the shore
Has just delivered a child
Cold blood wells from the stone
The tame heart's been driven wild.

Deep in the frozen heart
A snowdrop in perfect flower
Some sort of happiness has
Been assembled out of fire.

With winter white on the ground
Stillness came down to her cry
In the stable something's been born
Has joined them all queueing to die.

Has joined our lively queue
That leads through a studded oakdoor
Where together in bed she and I
Conceive the next fallen star.

Three Notes

I'll leave the door open
If there's no sign of me
Unlatch the windows
The evening's so silent
You can hear the gulls call
And down the valley the sea –
Follow the surf-fall
You'll find me.

Love, the door's on the latch
If I'm already gone
Feel at home, go upstairs –
When the valley is quiet
Breathe through the dark window
The tide's deepening song.
Sunrise tomorrow
I'll be home.

I've left our house open
If I'm not back tonight
Unlatch the window
Let the dark garden in –
The full moon, the owl's screech –
When that last star's taken flight
We'll meet on the beach
At first light.

First Light

When we were young, my lovely,
When the light looked over our trees,
Each day in the valley was sun-up,
A white blossom for the black honey-bees.

Or frost in gold October
Our old heron creaked up the stream,
A smile for the three old chinamen
Locked into our ageless dream.

We'd sit easy with death at table,
My skeleton key in the glass,
And whichever name he whispered
We'd both wait for the shiver to pass.

One day comes icy December
I see your hair turn grey,
Cold light on the kitchen table
Where the snowdrop petals lay.

For nights the stream stands frozen,
Our oakwood is stripped to the bone –
Just one of us stirs from the table,
It's death checking out of our home.

I looked but I couldn't find you
Then full-moon, the first summer breeze,
Came running through our garden
A white blossom for the black honey-bees.

Winter nights when our heron creaks over
We'll let the sand-glass run
To a blizzard of white cherry blossom
That melts in the morning sun.

Winter Solstice

I

Night. Her warm breath, its velvet touch, woke me. Dark breath
Scattering dark – she always beside me, asleep.
The drawl of surf
Dreams the valley – a form of breathing. This one Deep,
The ocean, unhealed, with no front or back – is birth ...
    is death.

Always the stream loudest in the still winter night –
No wind to ripple the black rain-barrel of stars.
Here sound is light,
Is the black light through space breathing open the bars,
The word whispered, the dark stream, and always the bird
    in flight.

Up from the deep ... No, I've nothing to say for love!
Complete out of the complete, the one missing line:
. . . .
Uttered in silence, the gold from the empty mine –
Word, image, form – on two conspiring wings the one
    paired dove.

Out from the deep love settles on a dying form –
Came crying to it, took on change, fell for the sky.
Bound to the storm,

We learn to feather, hover, in due time to die.
When featherbeds grow cold, somehow in her the heart's
    kept warm.

I touch her barely, can still feel the shape of love.
Our child. Children. Shared moments. Any little room.
My hawk ... my dove.
In umpteen upturned cups the Dharmakaya Moon ...
In her I cannot conceive anything − except it's love.

Her breath, the scent of it snatches me back; 'Firewood,'
I hear the Zen master say, 'is firewood. Ash ash.'
Half understood.
But how could her first light step on the terrace flash
Then and now our appointment. Can one now be now
    for good?

Love cuts through time, makes now the moment she first smiled −
This moment convenes one healed substance out of two:
My tame, her wild.
Alloy of life and death, its shape the standard due:
A child each moment, each moment our constant smiling child.

2

Then it was summer − mock-orange, mown hay. Some nights
I'd hear on the lawn him tiptoe the brink of dream
Towards first light.
Sea tangled with stars, the ripples on the dark stream
His laughter. The boy has opened his hand, the lark's in flight.

The song his, but the singing's ours − our love, his need.
Her nightdress dawn silver-grey, with little flowers ...
So we agreed.

A child conceived in heaven. That heaven was ours.
We'd made a bed of it, drilled the word love into the seed.

Afterwards she'd sleep. I'd watch day colour her lips.
Listen for his name, breathe the milk on her breath, touch
With fingertip
Her eyelids, see them flicker, see her smile, there catch
A moment the unspoken name – there let the moment slip.

I've read, 'As soon as one wave moves, ten thousand waves
Come following.' Thought on thought. Day after day. Though
Each moment lives
Its own? She sings, sews, heals a broken wing. I know
The timeless touch. Giving is what she gave, is what she gives.

The gift is life. I new-coined from our bed would run
Outdoors . . . light-threads from the ripped-cloth roar of the sea.
Each day first born.
The garden gleamed the dew – pond, the woods, each oaktree
Drenched in gold, glimmer of goldleaf in the first spray of sun.

Word by word we allowed summer to come and go –
Gorse-scent drifts from the cliff, haze, fields of yellow corn,
The lone swallow . . .
Behind each word a child. Behind each little song,
Each rose, the unknowing that holds us, knows, needs
      us to know.

Suddenly I'm breathing winter. All is heartbreak –
The last cherry-leaf falls, and look, I've dropped my pen . . .
Of course I ache . . .
If love is to let go I've still lessons to learn.
What I love is summer. White clouds. Winter . . . winter's
      the wake.

3

Ready, were we, for winter? You, not I. Instead
I, in the labour ward, expected summer song.
'A child born dead.'
I listened . . . listen. Then you say, 'A child is born.'
I hear distantly snow falling in the woods. The sky's lead.

So summers end – the yellow path into the trees.
Try in my hut to outstare winter's stare. Quick tears
Begin to freeze.
In ice I keep her soft heart beating. The he hears
Nothing. Then hears the mid-winter stream. Sees nothing,
  then sees

The girl, the brown girl far side of the frozen stream,
Hazel leaf in the ice-floe wind flash purest gold.
The vision-gleam –
Her half-smile fired and refetched in ice to unfold
Out of mind and time, dawn-dusk, drawn from the cambric
  of dream.

Frozen days I heard the thunder of this river.
Or nights , when out of pain love had fallen asleep,
Felt the quiver
Of colour, saw out of her brown almond eyes leap
The song's lightning, felt it run through me – like a love-shiver.

Light and shade, two women then, the river between –
Broken child/flawed poem, two voices out of key.
Their quarrelling
All my gift – I cradled the warring twins in me.
Face to face. O when was love ever a divided thing?

Listen ... she's dreaming. The stream, it's so loud tonight.
Ice, a thin lens on black winter's barrel of stars.
Her breath is light,
Black light singing through space, breathing open the bars –
A boy's name half-heard, the dark stream, always the bird
    in flight.

Spring came two-faced. Thorns – black and white for Eastertide.
The white the bone, white the blameless snow; white is death,
White is the bride.
Blackthorn the black, the Easter grave ... I catch my breath,
Black Magdalen! So He was crossed in love, me too ...
    crucified.

4

Summer's this tense affair. Baked hay-meadows steaming
Between the woods. The air inflamed. Dry crickets spark
    into kindling.
Leaf-tremble tells where she's watching us from the dark.
Plum-black the thunder clouds rumble the August evening.

My mother died. She lay full-dressed, full-summer dead.
Her son stands wondering – so she's been taken by storm.
I by her bed
Wondering where am I, where on earth has she gone ...
Stars hidden, space black, the earth transparent, life ... a
    snapped thread.

I dreamed a House of Women, sat all to their meal.
A boy-child played in the door – we two held from harm,
Allowed to heal.
The dark daughter got up to leave, she touched my arm,
Said before long we'd meet again – so would I learn to feel.

woke weeping . . . O without her there is no heart,
There is no feeling, no love – only this vacuum.
Set love apart
And it mirrors back to God his own abstraction.
It's she embodies the child-longing deep in God's own heart.

Crucible, where two make one. Soror Mystica . . .
Her smile the secret recipe. Queen Dakini
Lights on Brahma
Like the Autumn moon. Bees drum as Kundalini
First dreams the Lotus Child in the downstairs Muladhara.

Until I'm her temple! Feel how she takes my hand.
I follow her blind, this dark fragrance on the stair –
Can understand
Her sense as each room opens – am at last aware
It's love has the seven tied muscles of my heart expand.

Moment of meltdown – she loosens the final veil.
In the dark, the monsoon rain, Corda Pavonis,
The peacock's tail
Now opens its thousand eyes in midnight's moonless
Firmament. We come blind to heaven, fingering her braille.

                5
Far-fetched this cold midnight? Not in our balanced bed,
Safe-sealed in dark by a magic diagram.
My cloven head
Finds in her healed heart the child, our talisman –
That gold ring exacts life from the divisions of the dead.

Tiresias among the shades, blind syzygy
That spells life; Circe's love that spells the dark way down.
Root of the tree –

Royal incest that first conceived the golden crown.
John Donne, I bow: 'Whatever dies was not mixed equally.'

Dionysus came to his senses in her school.
He died dismembered – she taught him to come again.
So broke the rule,
Apollo's rule, with her life in the round. And then
She could milk them both, birth the two-faced child to end
    their duel.

The child that's made for life. Once in our double bed
She spoke from dream. I'd been awake, questioning God's sex.
'In God,' she said,
'Doing and being become synonymous,' The equal mix!
I laughed. Eureka! She'd hit the nail, me too, on the head.

Next dream was mine. I've come home – though this
    sunlit home
Clearly is hers. Cottage garden, slate roof, the walls
All built of stone.
The frontdoor open and she upstairs. When she calls
I see a meal laid for two in the little downstairs room.

The two become the four (become the rumoured eight).
O love, your smile – it strikes me, that deep-mingled look,
Illiterate.
The one smile Dante found that can't be brought to book –
Set in Mona Lisa's gaze the marriage is consummate.

Above: beneath. And as without within. The four
Become the two, two three. The third? It's youth, the stuff
That *will* endure.
Love, child of two: myself that's more than I . . . Enough!
One wholemeal loaf – that when we share it only makes
    for more.

6

Then in your fourfold arms with darkness off the latch
I'm drenched in a scent of hyacinth like blue rain –
And at that touch
Through the pearled mist our blackbird starts to sing again.
The purple juice! I drink, then as the vision stirs I watch.

Green fronds of budded beech flow with the April breeze:
Her white calico slip is drawn across my face.
And next her blouse –
Unbuttoned as the ferns unfurl. Her touch is traced
In everything – a leaf her lip, her breast a swarm of bees.

Then what's with winter? Widow-fetch with her burden
Of damp sticks, bent in the snow-flecked gale – Death's shadow
In our garden.
I shrink till eyes can wrest from the black-out pillow
Only this dancing girl, her hair adaze with apple blossom.

So death too, two-faced. Two-scented death – the white rose,
The dank tomb. Even death reflects life's double-bind.
(Though there are those,
Yeats, Balthus, trick death with the girl they leave behind.
At sixty perhaps best to dream – and keep one nostril closed!)

O Love, what gives with this winter? October mild,
December cold. Contrary storms. The fire, the ice –
Unreconciled.
Mismatched. But fix him full-circle the cockatrice
Can heal. The mid-winter coffin cradles Mid-winter's child.

Winter's a double bed bound by our wedding ring.
The golden line of sunset in the winter sky
Is still your hem.

Ice on the written stone the cold sheen to our joy.
The frozen earth-scent of winter, the first milk-breath of spring.

Now. Always now. Life and death. Remember how Dogen
By *his* dead mother watched smoke from the joss-stick clear,
Drift into Zen –
Felt loss become such deep loneliness, year on year
Deepen, until loneliness emptied out the mind . . . Amen.

7

Such noble loneliness . . . it chills me to the bone:
Warrior's Sacred Path, the Bodhisattva Way.
Left on my own
I make for your eyes . . . love's so simple, it's child's play . . .
Down in our garden a child laughs . . . we're no longer alone.

Even Midnight, Dogen says, already it's dawn.
I breathe the dark, the light. So old crocked legs, that's how
Headlong you run
To her still down through the bluebell woods. And that's how
One star still can spark the crib in our cud-sweet, pregnant barn.

Our child's the presence that predicates the Other.
So waking to find your head sharing my pillow's
A metaphor

For God. Which means that every given name hallows
Our bed. Love never came up with love – without a lover.

It also means each breath's the moment I expire,
Then wake to find your head on my pillow, your gaze –
First-morning fire
Reflected in your smile, us two drawn to the blaze,
Little birds who shed their shadow in the Simurgh's pyre.

Listen, the streams . . . the sea breathing. O Omega!
O bright stars, paled in the black rain-barrel of night,
Drawn together
Out of time and down to our pinpoint now of light.
O Alpha! Love each moment's a starfall cast forever.

It's now you breathe, you sleep, you stir – it's now you wake.
Look: nightdress, silver-grey with summer's flowers . . . dawn
About to break.
Listen! Already the blackbird singing. His song
Is now, is light – he sings our universe, the whole heart-ache.

Suzuki's Timeless Spring, Trungpa's Great Eastern Sun . . .
Thunder of grass, or dawn's wild drum-beat in the sky . . .
All *now*. John Donne,

My thanks – 'Whatever dies was not mixed equally.'
My partner then? Yes Love, yes now – *our* dance. It's just
begun.

Notes

1 Form and Rhyme

Overture: 15 lines, any length or strain – and three rhymes, set as it were symmetrically except for a recapitulation before the end: AABACBBACBC/ABC/C.

Skeleton Key: 3 stanzas, each 21 syllables in 3 lines, with rhyme or1/2-rhyme scheme ABA CBC ABA.

The Ballad of the Leat: Each rhyme established then yielding to the next (ABBA BCCB CDDC ...) intended to imitate the down-the- stream sound of water!

Practice: a far-fetched version of a Li Po 'sonnet' – after reading Arthur Cooper's introduction to his translations of Li Po. This version has four 8/7 couplets (somehow the Chinese can operate on 2/3) with a concealed rhyme or 1/2-rhyme (sometimes as little as a vowel echo) scheme:

```
        8------
        7-----A
        8------
        7--B---

        8------
        7--A---
        8------
        7------B
```

2 *Reverie For Child and Garden:* The form drawn from The Gospel of Buddha, which suggests five stages of meditation: on love for all beings, on pity, on joy, on impurity, and on serene detachment.

3 *Fiesta:* The question stands – just who at the *fiesta* is being honoured by the dancing? Orthodox ritual is observed, if innocently embroidered. Innocently? While lip-service is being paid to the new Lord, the Christian Sun-tyrant, that which the dancers worship is all that has gone to earth – the Moon, the ancient intuitive life, magic and the thousand eyes of night.

4 *Wendy's Song:* Wendy Ann Mitchell, poet, was fiancée to the bird-warden on Lundy Island. She slipped and fell past him on to the rocks and was killed. She was, I think, twenty. The couplet which ends each stanza, and so hauntingly catches the mood of Lundy, is hers. I came across it, cut in a free-standing flat-stone epitaph that had been left, at random it seemed, somewhere on the spine of the island. The last time I visited, the epitaph had gone – I imagine to the weather.

5 *Genesis:* The idea being that The Creation is a drama of self-realization, a *tantric* exercise in which the wakening energy is allowed to mount through the houses of the seven chakras to perfection, or Enlightenment. Or the completion of the Work.

Soahum – 'the supreme mantra of non-duality', a Sanskrit word meaning something like, *I am that* – and so, *I am everything.*

6 *Milarepa and the Five Wisdoms:* In his book *Cutting Through Spiritual Materialism,* Chögyam Trungpa writes, 'In the Tantric tradition energy is categorized in five basic qualities or *Buddha Families: Vajra, Ratna, Padma, Karma* and *Buddha.* Each Buddha Family has an emotion associated with it which is transmuted into a particular 'wisdom' or aspect of the awakened state of mind. The Buddha Families are also associated with colours, elements, landscapes, directions, seasons, with any aspect of the phenomenal world.'

The associated emotions are as follows, *Vajra* – anger, *Ratna* pride, *Padma* – passion and possessiveness, *Karma* – envy, *Buddha* – dullness, And these are realized in the awakened state as, respectively, Mirror-like Wisdom, Equanimity. Discriminating Awareness, All-Accomplishing Action and All-Encompassing Space. Thus Buddha can be seen as the 'basic ground', the environment or oxygen that makes it possible for the other principles to function.

Milarepa, poet of *The Hundred Thousand Songs,* became the *Vidyadhara* or 'Holder of the Crazy Wisdom', and as such a personification of Enlightenment through Tantra.

7 *Winter Solstice:* the night soliloquy, it harks back to the earlier *Stages of Solar Eclipse,* and so becomes the second episode of *the*

mind awake while she sleeps. Several images are developed, key to not just the two poems, but to the collection as a whole: the sea, the stream, the garden, the bird, the marriage bed, the lost child, and the child found, the brown Arab girl – intended (I suppose) as a complete metaphysics. The poem then, in fact and in imagination, and within the gnosis of its own making, is a gathering of threads.

Most of the references to names and myths earn their keep by resonance alone, but are easily enough researched for fuller meaning. Maybe one or two require a note.

1/5 *Dharmakaya* (literally, *body of truth*), in Buddhism it relates to the original state of being: complete openness, complete spaciousness, complete generosity.

7/4 *Simurgh*, the fiery City of God, and the end of the journey in *The Conference of the Birds* by the great 12th-century Sufi poet, Attar.

7/5 *Omega*, in my mind a direct reference to its use at the end of *Stages of Solar Eclipse*, and so in part to the specific vision of Teilhard de Chardin for whom Omega is, if I've caught it right, the fulfilment of evolution in the universal realization of love.

7/7 Shunryu Suzuki and Chögyam Trungpa – the sense is intended to spring from a personal acknowledgement. Because their writing has stayed fresh and in daily use for me for so long I've become devoted to each of them – as endlessly inept student to infinitely patient friend.

Also by John Moat

POETRY

Thunder of Grass
6d per per annum
Skeleton Key
Fiesta & Fox Reviews His Prophecy
The Welcombe Overtures
Firewater & The Miraculous Mandarin
Practice (with drawings)
The Valley (with drawings)

NOVELS

Heorot
Bartonwoold
Mai's Wedding
The Missing Moon

Also
A Standard of Verse
and with John Fairfax
The Way to Write